# THOMAS HARDY'S
# CHOSEN POEMS

THOMAS HARDY

# THOMAS HARDY'S CHOSEN POEMS

Edited by Francine Shapiro Puk

FREDERICK UNGAR PUBLISHING CO.

# CONTENTS

## PART I

### POEMS CHIEFLY LYRICAL

v

# CONTENTS

# CONTENTS

## PART II

### POEMS NARRATIVE AND REFLECTIVE

## PART III

### WAR POEMS, AND LYRICS FROM "THE DYNASTS"

# APPENDIX I

## CRITICAL ADDITIONS

## APPENDIX II

### POEMS OF 1912–13

# CONTENTS

# INTRODUCTION

The renewed critical acclaim for Thomas Hardy during the fiftieth anniversary of his death in 1978 marked a change in the slow decline of interest in his novels after 1928. But the diminished attention to Hardy the novelist in the decades following his death opened the way for a re-evaluation of Hardy the poet, and it was as a poet that Hardy meant to be best remembered. A new biography, a collection of letters, critical studies, and a new collected edition of his poetry contributed to a "Hardy renaissance"—leading to a wider audience for one of England's, and the world's, major novelists and poets. As if to cap the resurgent interest, some of the novels themselves were dramatized for television in Great Britain and the United States.

During Hardy's long life—he died at the age of 88—he published fourteen novels, set in the southwestern part of England that he called Wessex, where he was born. The best-known and most successful of his novels were *The Return of the Native, The Mayor of Casterbridge, Tess of the D'Urbervilles*, and *Jude the Obscure*. Despite their great popularity, the latter two were violently denounced as depicting indecency and immorality. As a consequence of this criticism, Hardy decided to write no more novels but to devote himself to poetry, which he had long preferred. His first book of verse, *Wessex Poems*, appeared in 1898. Seven more followed, as did *The Dynasts*, an epic drama on the Napoleonic Wars. The last volume of poetry, *Winter*

*Words*, was published in October, 1928, nine months after his death.

In 1929 a new selection of Hardy's poetry was issued under the title *Chosen Poems of Thomas Hardy*. Essentially it was a revision of the *Selected Poems* (1916), and Hardy had hoped the volume would reach a larger audience. Prepared during the final year of his life and submitted to the publisher only four months before his death, *Chosen Poems* was Hardy's last major project, his final word on what constitutes a representative sampling of his poetic canon. These poems form the bulk of the present volume.

The 161 poems and songs that Hardy selected for *Chosen Poems* display his unique qualities. A master of Victorian artistry, he depicts man's obsessive self-consciousness in "these disordered years of our prematurely afflicted century." He is similar to Browning in his steadfast insistence that his poetry was to be regarded as "dramatic monologues by different characters." The language of his narrators vividly creates individuals who are distinct in personality, social class, and self-awareness. For example, the presumptuous egotist of "A Broken Appointment" is a vivid contrast to the weary philosopher of "Before and After Summer" and to the haunted psyche in "Wessex Heights." Although there are autobiographical aspects to these and other narrators, they are as much poetic creations as the speakers of "A Trampwoman's Tragedy" and "The Burghers." Hardy's emphasis is not on the philosophy, but on the narrator's inability to view his situation objectively and to foresee the consequences of his actions.

The poetry is deliberately patterned after the rhythm of colloquial speech, although the narrative is textured by inverted syntax, coined words, metrical shifts, and musical cadences. The purpose is to wed "sound and sense" so as to recreate the drama of experience. The lyric swing of "Amabel" sweeps the narrator from his attachment to the past with a measure as steady and inexorable as a pendulum. In "A Broken Appointment," the deadening misery of time's slow pace is driven home by the staccato measure of the *repeton:* "You did not come."

Hardy never uses free verse, but rather manipulates

form, meter, and imagery within a traditional framework. The difference between the first and last stanzas of "The Going" provides a good illustration of his mastery:

Why did you give no hint that night
That quickly after the morrow's dawn,
And calmly, as if indifferent quite,
You would close your term here, up and be gone
      Where I could not follow
      With wing of swallow
To gain one glimpse of you ever anon !
. . . . . . . . . . . . . . . . . . . . . . . . . . . . . . . . . . . . . . . . . . . .
      Well, well !   All's past amend,
      Unchangeable.   It must go.
I seem but a dead man held on end
To sink down soon. . . . O you could not know
      That such swift fleeing
      No soul foreseeing—
Not even I—would undo me so!

Both are precise seven line stanzas with parallel rhyme. However, the regular meter and traditional imagery of the searching opening lines are radically altered to the contracted form of the final stanza, with its slow measure and its image of total dissolution. Hardy's craft sufficiently integrates these widely disparate stanzas within the poem so as to give the impression of organic continuity.

Throughout his poetry, Hardy succeeds in linking the narratively unified images with an art so refined as to conceal itself. Great care is taken to make each seemingly self-contained stanza an intimately connected element of a unified whole. His intricate manipulation can be seen in the repeated double rhymes of the contracted fifth and sixth lines of each stanza of "The Going." Other examples are found in his use of *terza rima** in "The Burghers" and

---

*Hardy's mastery of this rarely used verse form is further evidenced in the endings he employs. The *terza rima* traditionally ends with either a couplet or a single line that rhymes with

"Friends Beyond" (where the second line of each tercet is picked up as the predominate rhyme in the following stanza), in "A Sheep Fair," where an end word is repeatedly rhymed in the ninth line of each stanza, and in "Beyond the Last Lamp," where the word "sadly" is repeated in the fourth line of each stanza. The connective devices serve as a parallel to the way the mind itself functions, slipping from one thought to another with an associative connection subliminally maintained. As such, the technique is perfectly suited to Hardy's presentation of the narrator's unfolding awareness through the very naturalness of its effect.

*Chosen Poems* opens with

> The eternal question of what Life was,
> And why we were there, and by whose strange laws
>     That which mattered most could not be.

And while there is no answer to this "eternal question," Hardy presents a panoramic view of characters intent on finding a solution. As his narrators strip themselves of their social masks, the reader is alerted to the common bonds of humanity, for the itinerant Trampwoman, the affluent Burgher, and the full spectrum of personae tell the story of man's dis-ease. Each character reveals Hardy's view that "delight is a delicate growth cramped by crookedness, custom, and fear." With the humanizing effect of his poetry, Hardy urges the reader to make his own philosophy out of his personal experience rather than be caught in the self-delusive postures of his narrators. He presents his vision not as a pessimist, but in the firm belief that "a full look at the Worst" is necessary if mankind is to progress. While the narrators succumb to an uncongenial uni-

---

the second line of the preceding tercet. Hardy, however, obtains a more symmetrical closure by ending "Friends Beyond" in a tercet that echoes the opening stanza, and in "The Burghers" by having the second line in the final tercet rhyme with lines one and three of the preceding stanza.

verse, the reader should attune himself to the poetry's underlying refrain:

> Let me enjoy the earth no less
> Because the all-enacting Might
> That fashioned forth its loveliness
> Had other aims than my delight.

As with few other poets, there is no critical consensus as to what constitutes Hardy's best work. The richness and variety of Hardy's some nine hundred poems make selection notoriously difficult. The subjective nature of each collection enhances the value of *Chosen Poems* as an important biographical document. In the fifty years since Hardy's death, however, critics have overlooked this volume in their own search for a definitive anthology. Not surprisingly, Hardy selected most of the poems his admirers have singled out. But the poems in the first appendix have been included so as not to deprive the reader of certain additional critical favorites. Books and articles dealing with Hardy's poetry have been examined to determine the poems most often cited as particularly striking for technique, beauty, or point of view. Not all of Hardy's poems have received unanimous praise, but *Chosen Poems* and the fourteen additional selections narrow the range to those most consistently thought to be his best.

A similar motive is behind the inclusion of the complete sequence of "Poems of 1912–13" in the second appendix. The poems that Hardy termed "an expiation" for his neglect of his first wife, and that he wrote during the months following her death, had special significance for the author. They were the only poems that Hardy explicitly labeled "personal" and he carefully arranged them to reflect a torturous psychic journey from despair to resigned acceptance.

The twenty-one poem sequence was published under the epigraph "Veteris vestigia flammae." The line is taken from Virgil's *Aeneid* (IV, 23) and is translated as "the traces of an ancient flame." The description is related to Dido who "long since wounded by the shafts of love, feeds

the wound with her life-blood; consumed with secret fire
. . . love's sickness grants her no repose." The narrator of
"Poems of 1912–13" reveals the same condition and ex-
plores the fire's "flickering."

The poems individually are no different in form or style
from the rest of the canon. However, the force of the cu-
mulative impression has caused the sequence to be cri-
tically acknowledged as one of the most moving experi-
ences in literature. To date, it has been printed in full only
in the massive collected editions and is consequently
known only to the initiates of the Hardy fellowship. But
"Poems of 1912–13" is an indispensable component of the
"essential" Hardy.

## TEXTUAL NOTE

Hardy's arrangement of *Chosen Poems* has been scrupu-
lously maintained in this volume. His three divisions un-
questionably facilitate the "right note-catching" that he
insisted on for a full understanding of his work. The poems
in the first appendix are chronologically arranged by the
volume in which they first appeared.

The variant readings found in *Chosen Poems* constitute
Hardy's final revision of his poetry. Notes on these revi-
sions and on the nine excerpts from *The Dynasts* and *The
Famous Tragedy of the Queen of Cornwall* follow the second
appendix. Three of the excerpted songs were added when
Hardy revised his *Selected Poems* and are unique to this
volume, not having been included in the otherwise com-
prehensive *Complete Poems*.

To provide greater access, the original index of first
lines has been supplemented by an index of titles. The sec-
ond index also indicates the volumes in which the poems
first appeared.

For further discussion on the significance of *Chosen
Poems*, the reader is referred to James Gibson's "The Po-
etic Text" in *Thomas Hardy and the Modern World* (1974),

edited by F. B. Pinion, and to *Thomas Hardy: A Bibliographical Study* (1954) by Richard L. Purdy. These scholars have laid the groundwork for any serious consideration of Hardy's art.

F.S.P.

# PART I

## POEMS CHIEFLY LYRICAL

# AFTER THE VISIT

### (To F. E. D.)

COME again to the place
Where your presence was as a leaf that skims
Down a drouthy way whose ascent bedims
    The bloom on the farer's face.

Come again, with the feet
That were light on the green as a thistledown
        ball,
And those mute ministrations to one and to all
    Beyond a man's saying sweet.

Until then the faint scent
Of the bordering flowers swam unheeded away,
And I marked not the charm in the changes of
        day
    As the cloud-colours came and went.

Through the dark corridors
Your walk was so soundless I did not know
Your form from a phantom's of long ago
    Said to pass on the ancient floors.

Till you drew from the shade,
And I saw the large luminous living eyes
Regard me in fixed inquiring-wise
    As those of a soul that weighed,

    Scarce consciously,
The eternal question of what Life was,
And why we were there, and by whose strange
        laws
    That which mattered most could not be.

# TO MEET, OR OTHERWISE

WHETHER to sally and see thee, girl of my
  dreams,
  Or whether to stay
And see thee not! How vast the difference
  seems
  Of Yea from Nay
Just now. Yet this same sun will slant its
  beams
  At no far day
On our two mounds, and then what will the
  difference weigh!

Yet I will see thee, maiden dear, and make
  The most I can
Of what remains to us amid this brake
  Cimmerian
Through which we grope, and from whose
  thorns we ache,
  While still we scan
Round our frail faltering progress for some path
  or plan.

By briefest meeting something sure is won;
  It will have been:

Nor God nor Demon can undo the done,
　　Unsight the seen,
Make muted music be as unbegun,
　　Though things terrene
Groan in their bondage till oblivion supervene.

So, to the one long-sweeping symphony
　　From times remote
Till now, of human tenderness, shall we
　　Supply one note,
Small and untraced, yet that will ever be
　　Somewhere afloat
Amid the spheres, as part of sick Life's antidote.

# THE DIFFERENCE

## I

SINKING down by the gate I discern the thin
    moon,
And a blackbird tries over old airs in the pine,
But the moon is a sorry one, sad the bird's
    tune,
For this spot is unknown to that Heartmate of
    mine.

## II

Did my Heartmate but haunt here at times
    such as now,
The song would be joyous and cheerful the
    moon ;
But she will see never this gate, path, or bough,
Nor I find a joy in the scene or the tune

# ON THE DEPARTURE PLATFORM

WE kissed at the barrier ; and passing through
She left me, and moment by moment got
Smaller and smaller, until to my view
    She was but a spot ;

A wee white spot of muslin fluff
That down the diminishing platform bore
Through hustling crowds of gentle and rough
    To the carriage door.

Under the lamplight's fitful glowers,
Behind dark groups from far and near,
Whose interests were apart from ours,
    She would disappear,

Then show again, till I ceased to see
That flexible form, that nebulous white ;
And she who was more than my life to me
    Had vanished quite. . . .

We have penned new plans since that fair fond
    day,
And in season she will appear again—

Perhaps in the same soft white array—
    But never as then !

—" And why, young man, must eternally fly
A joy you'll repeat, if you love her well ? "
—O friend, nought happens twice thus ;  why,
    I cannot tell !

# IN A CATHEDRAL CITY

THESE people have not heard your name ;
No loungers in this placid place
Have helped to bruit your beauty's fame.

The grey Cathedral, towards whose face
Bend eyes untold, has met not yours ;
Your shade has never swept its base,

Your form has never darked its doors,
Nor have your faultless feet once thrown
A pensive pit-pat on its floors.

Along the street to maids well known
Blithe lovers hum their tender airs,
But in your praise voice not a tone. . . .

—Since nought bespeaks you here, or bears,
As I, your imprint through and through,
Here might I rest, till my heart shares
The spot's unconsciousness of you !

SALISBURY.

## "I SAY I'LL SEEK HER"

I SAY, " I'll seek her side
    Ere hindrance interposes ";
    But eve in midnight closes,
And here I still abide.

When darkness wears I see
    Her sad eyes in a vision ;
    They ask, " What indecision
Detains you, Love, from me ?—

" The creaking hinge is oiled,
    I have unbarred the backway,
    But you tread not the trackway ;
And shall the thing be spoiled ?

" Far cockcrows echo shrill,
    The shadows are abating,
    And I am waiting, waiting ;
But O, you tarry still ! "

# SONG OF HOPE

O SWEET To-morrow ! —
  After to-day
  There will away
This sense of sorrow.
Then let us borrow
Hope, for a gleaming
Soon will be streaming,
  Dimmed by no gray —
  No gray !

While the winds wing us
  Sighs from The Gone,
  Nearer to dawn
Minute-beats bring us ;
When there will sing us
Larks, of a glory
Waiting our story
  Further anon —
  Anon !

Doff the black token,
  Don the red shoon,
  Right and retune
Viol-strings broken ;

Null the words spoken
In speeches of rueing,
The night cloud is hueing,
     To-morrow shines soon—
          Shines soon !

# BEFORE AND AFTER SUMMER

## I

Looking forward to the spring
One puts up with anything.
On this February day
Though the winds leap down the street
Wintry scourgings seem but play,
And these later shafts of sleet
—Sharper pointed than the first—
And these later snows—the worst—
Are as a half-transparent blind
Riddled by rays from sun behind.

## II

Shadows of the October pine
Reach into this room of mine :
On the pine there swings a bird ;
He is shadowed with the tree.
Mutely perched he bills no word ;
Blank as I am even is he.
For those happy suns are past,
Fore-discerned in winter last.
When went by their pleasure, then ?
I, alas, perceived not when.

# FIRST SIGHT OF HER AND AFTER

A DAY is drawing to its fall
    I had not dreamed to see ;
The first of many to enthrall
    My spirit, will it be ?
Or is this eve the end of all
    Such new delight for me ?

I journey home : the pattern grows
    Of moonshades on the way :
" Soon the first quarter, I suppose,"
    Sky-glancing travellers say ;
I realize that it, for those,
    Has been a common day.

# THE SUN ON THE BOOKCASE

*(Student's Love-song* : 1870)

ONCE more the cauldron of the sun
Smears the bookcase with winy red,
And here my page is, and there my bed,
And the apple-tree shadows travel along.
Soon their intangible track will be run,
   And dusk grow strong
   And they have fled.

Yes : now the boiling ball is gone,
And I have wasted another day. . . .
But wasted—*wasted*, do I say ?
Is it a waste to have imaged one
Beyond the hills there, who, anon,
   My great deeds done,
   Will be mine alway ?

# "WHEN I SET OUT FOR LYONNESSE"

(1870)

WHEN I set out for Lyonnesse,
　　A hundred miles away,
　　The rime was on the spray,
And starlight lit my lonesomeness
When I set out for Lyonnesse
　　A hundred miles away.

What would bechance at Lyonnesse
　　While I should sojourn there
　　No prophet durst declare,
Nor did the wisest wizard guess
What would bechance at Lyonnesse
　　While I should sojourn there.

When I came back from Lyonnesse
　　With magic in my eyes,
　　All marked with mute surmise
My radiance rare and fathomless,
When I came back from Lyonnesse
　　With magic in my eyes!

17

# AT THE WORD "FAREWELL"

SHE looked like a bird from a cloud
  On the clammy lawn,
Moving alone, bare-browed
  In the dim of dawn.
The candles alight in the room
  For my parting meal
Made all things withoutdoors loom
  Strange, ghostly, unreal.

The hour itself was a ghost,
  And it seemed to me then
As of chances the chance furthermost
  I should see her again.
I beheld not where all was so fleet
  That a Plan of the past
Which had ruled us from birthtime to meet
  Was in working at last :

No prelude did I there perceive
  To a drama at all,
Or foreshadow what fortune might weave
  From beginnings so small ;

But I rose as if quicked by a spur
  I was bound to obey,
And stepped through the casement to her
  Still alone in the gray.

" I am leaving you. . . . Farewell ! " I said,
  As I followed her on
By an alley bare boughs overspread ;
  " I soon must be gone ! "
Even then the scale might have been turned
  Against love by a feather,
—But crimson one cheek of hers burned
  When we came in together.

# DITTY

(E. L. G.)

BENEATH a knap where flown
      Nestlings play,
Within walls of weathered stone,
      Far away
From the files of formal houses,
By the bough the firstling browses,
Lives a Sweet : no merchants meet,
No man barters, no man sells
      Where she dwells.

Upon that fabric fair
      " Here is she ! "
Seems written everywhere
      Unto me.
But to friends and nodding neighbours,
Fellow-wights in lot and labours,
Who descry the times as I,
No such lucid legend tells
      Where she dwells.

Should I lapse to what I was
      Ere we met ;

(Such will not be, but because
      Some forget
Let me feign it)—none would notice
That where she I know by rote is
Spread a strange and withering change,
Like a drying of the wells
      Where she dwells.

To feel I might have kissed—
      Loved as true—
Otherwhere, nor Mine have missed
      My life through,
Had I never wandered near her,
Is a smart severe—severer
In the thought that she is nought,
Even as I, beyond the dells
      Where she dwells.

And Devotion droops her glance
      To recall
What bond-servants of Chance
      We are all.
I but found her in that, going
On my errant path unknowing,
I did not out-skirt the spot
That no spot on earth excels,
      —Where she dwells !

1870.

# THE NIGHT OF THE DANCE

THE cold moon hangs to the sky by its horn,
    And centres its gaze on me ;
The stars, like eyes in reverie,
Their westering as for a while forborne,
    Quiz downward curiously.

Old Robert draws the backbrand in,
    The green logs steam and spit ;
The half-awakened sparrows flit
From the riddled thatch ; and owls begin
    To whoo from the gable-slit.

Yes ; far and nigh things seem to know
    Sweet scenes are impending here ;
That all is prepared ; that the hour is near
For welcomes, fellowships, and flow
    Of sally, song, and cheer ;

That spigots are pulled and viols strung ;
    That soon will arise the sound
Of measures trod to tunes renowned ;
That She will return in Love's low tongue
    My vows as we wheel around.

# TO LIZBIE BROWNE

## I

Dear Lizbie Browne,
Where are you now?
In sun, in rain?—
Or is your brow
Past joy, past pain,
Dear Lizbie Browne?

## II

Sweet Lizbie Browne,
How you could smile,
How you could sing!—
How archly wile
In glance-giving,
Sweet Lizbie Browne!

## III

And, Lizbie Browne,
Who else had hair
Bay-red as yours,

23

Or flesh so fair
Bred out of doors,
Sweet Lizbie Browne ?


### IV

When, Lizbie Browne,
You had just begun
To be endeared
By stealth to one,
You disappeared
My Lizbie Browne !


### V

Ay, Lizbie Browne,
So swift your life,
And mine so slow,
You were a wife
Ere I could show
Love, Lizbie Browne.


### VI

Still, Lizbie Browne,
You won, they said,
The best of men
When you were wed. . . .
Where went you then,
O Lizbie Browne ?

## VII

Dear Lizbie Browne,
I should have thought,
" Girls ripen fast,"
And coaxed and caught
You ere you passed,
Dear Lizbie Browne !

## VIII

But, Lizbie Browne,
I let you slip ;
Shaped not a sign ;
Touched never your lip
With lip of mine,
Lost Lizbie Browne !

## IX

So, Lizbie Browne,
When on a day
Men speak of me
As not, you'll say,
" And who was he ? "—
Yes, Lizbie Browne !

# LET ME ENJOY

### I

LET me enjoy the earth no less
Because the all-enacting Might
That fashioned forth its loveliness
Had other aims than my delight.

### II

About my path there flits a Fair,
Who throws me not a word or sign ;
I'll charm me with her ignoring air,
And laud the lips not meant for mine.

### III

From manuscripts of moving song
Inspired by scenes and dreams unknown
I'll pour out raptures that belong
To others, as they were my own.

### IV

And some day hence, toward Paradise
And all its blest—if such should be—
I will lift glad, afar-off eyes,
Though it contain no place for me.

# THE BALLAD-SINGER

Sing, Ballad-singer, raise a hearty tune ;
Make me forget that there was ever a one
I walked with in the meek light of the moon
    When the day's work was done.

Rhyme, Ballad-rhymer, start a country song ;
Make me forget that she whom I loved well
Swore she would love me dearly, love me long,
    Then—what I cannot tell !

Sing, Ballad-singer, from your little book ;
Make me forget those heart-breaks, achings,
    fears ;
Make me forget her name, her sweet sweet
    look—
    Make me forget her tears.

# THE DIVISION

RAIN on the windows, creaking doors,
    With blasts that besom the green,
And I am here, and you are there,
    And a hundred miles between !

O were it but the weather, Dear,
    O were it but the miles
That summed up all our severance,
    There might be room for smiles.

But that thwart thing betwixt us twain,
    Which nothing cleaves or clears,
Is more than distance, Dear, or rain,
    And longer than the years !

1893.

# YELL'HAM-WOOD'S STORY

COOMB-FIRTREES say that Life is a moan,
    And Clyffe-hill Clump says " Yea ! "
But Yell'ham says a thing of its own :
        It's not " Gray, gray
        Is Life alway ! "
        That Yell'ham says.
    Nor that Life is for ends unknown.

It says that Life would signify
    A thwarted purposing :
That we come to live, and are called to die.
        Yes, that's the thing
        In fall, in spring,
        That Yell'ham says :—
    " Life offers—to deny ! "

1902.

# HER INITIALS

Upon a poet's page I wrote
Of old two letters of her name ;
Part seemed she of the effulgent thought
Whence that high singer's rapture came.
—When now I turn the leaf the same
Immortal light illumes the lay,
But from the letters of her name
The radiance has waned away !

1869.

## THE WOUND

I CLIMBED to the crest,
 And, fog-festooned,
The sun lay west
 Like a crimson wound :

Like that wound of mine
 Of which none knew,
For I'd given no sign
 That it pierced me through

# HAP

I<small>F</small> but some vengeful god would call to me
From up the sky, and laugh : '' Thou suffering
    thing,
Know that thy sorrow is my ecstasy,
That thy love's loss is my hate's profiting ! ''

Then would I bear it, clench myself, and die,
Steeled by the sense of ire unmerited ;
Half-eased in that a Powerfuller than I
Had willed and meted me the tears I shed.

But not so.    How arrives it joy lies slain,
And why unblooms the best hope ever sown ?
—Crass Casualty obstructs the sun and rain,
And dicing Time for gladness casts a moan. . . .
These purblind Doomsters had as readily strown
Blisses about my pilgrimage as pain.

1866.

# A MERRYMAKING IN QUESTION

" I WILL get a new string for my fiddle,
     And call to the neighbours to come,
And partners shall dance down the middle
     Until the old pewter-wares hum :
     And we'll sip the mead, cyder, and rum ! "

From the night came the oddest of answers :
     A hollow wind, like a bassoon,
And headstones all ranged up as dancers,
     And cypresses droning a croon,
     And gurgoyles that mouthed to the tune.

## " HOW GREAT MY GRIEF "

### (TRIOLET)

How great my grief, my joys how few,
    Since first it was my fate to know thee !
—Have the slow years not brought to view
How great my grief, my joys how few,
Nor memory shaped old times anew,
    Nor loving-kindness helped to show thee
How great my grief, my joys how few,
    Since first it was my fate to know thee ?

# AT AN INN

WHEN we as strangers sought
    Their catering care,
Veiled smiles bespoke their thought
    Of what we were.
They warmed as they opined
    Us more than friends—
That we had all resigned
    For love's dear ends.

And that swift sympathy
    With living love
Which quicks the world—maybe
    The spheres above,
Made them our ministers,
    Moved them to say,
" Ah, God, that bliss like theirs
    Would flush our day ! "

And we were left alone
    As Love's own pair ;
Yet never the love-light shone
    Between us there !

But that which chilled the breath
     Of afternoon,
And palsied unto death
     The pane-fly's tune.

The kiss their zeal foretold,
     And now deemed come,
Came not : within his hold
     Love lingered numb.
Why cast he on our port
     A bloom not ours ?
Why shaped us for his sport
     In after-hours ?

As we seemed we were not
     That day afar,
And now we seem not what
     We aching are.
O severing sea and land,
     O laws of men,
Ere death, once let us stand
     As we stood then !

# A BROKEN APPOINTMENT

You did not come,
And marching Time drew on, and wore me
 numb.—
Yet less for loss of your dear presence there
Than that I thus found lacking in your make
That high compassion which can overbear
Reluctance for pure lovingkindness' sake
Grieved I, when, as the hope-hour stroked its
 sum,
You did not come.

You love not me,
And love alone can lend you loyalty ;
—I know and knew it.   But, unto the store
Of human deeds divine in all but name,
Was it not worth a little hour or more
To add yet this : Once you, a woman, came
To soothe a time-torn man ; even though it be
You love not me ?

# THOUGHTS OF PHENA

## AT NEWS OF HER DEATH

NOT a line of her writing have I,
Not a thread of her hair,
No mark of her late time as dame in her dwelling,
whereby
I may picture her there ;
And in vain do I urge my unsight
To conceive my lost prize
At her close, whom I knew when her dreams
were upbrimming with light,
And with laughter her eyes.

What scenes spread around her last days,
Sad, shining, or dim ?
Did her gifts and compassions enray and enarch
her sweet ways
With an aureate nimb ?
Or did life-light decline from her years,
And mischances control
Her full day-star ; unease, or regret, or fore-
bodings, or fears
Disennoble her soul ?

Thus I do but the phantom retain
    Of the maiden of yore
As my relic ; yet haply the best of her—fined
    in my brain
    It may be the more
That no line of her writing have I,
    Nor a thread of her hair,
No mark of her late time as dame in her dwelling,
    whereby
    I may picture her there.

*March* 1890.

## IN A EWELEAZE NEAR
## WEATHERBURY

THE years have gathered grayly
   Since I danced upon this leaze
With one who kindled gaily
   Love's fitful ecstasies !
But despite the term as teacher,
   I remain what I was then
In each essential feature
   Of the fantasies of men.

Yet I note the little chisel
   Of never-napping Time
Defacing wan and grizzel
   The blazon of my prime.
When at night he thinks me sleeping
   I feel him boring sly
Within my bones, and heaping
   Quaintest pains for by-and-by.

Still, I'd go the world with Beauty,
   I would laugh with her and sing,
I would shun divinest duty
   To resume her worshipping.
But she'd scorn my brave endeavour,
   She would not balm the breeze
By murmuring " Thine for ever ! "
   As she did upon this leaze.

1890.

# A SPOT

In years defaced and lost,
Two sat here, transport-tossed,
Lit by a living love
The wilted world knew nothing of :
    Scared momently
    By gaingivings,
    Then hoping things
    That could not be. . . .

Of love and us no trace
Abides upon the place ;
The sun and shadows wheel,
Season and season sereward steal ;
    Foul days and fair
    Here, too, prevail,
    And gust and gale
    As everywhere.

But lonely shepherd souls
Who bask amid these knolls
May catch a faery sound
On sleepy noontides from the ground :
    " O not again
    Till Earth outwears
    Shall love like theirs
    Suffuse this glen ! "

41

# THE DARKLING THRUSH

I LEANT upon a coppice gate
    When Frost was spectre-gray,
And Winter's dregs made desolate
    The weakening eye of day.
The tangled bine-stems scored the sky
    Like strings of broken lyres,
And all mankind that haunted nigh
    Had sought their household fires.

The land's sharp features seemed to be
    The Century's corpse outleant,
His crypt the cloudy canopy,
    The wind his death-lament.
The ancient pulse of germ and birth
    Was shrunken hard and dry,
And every spirit upon earth
    Seemed fervourless as I.

At once a voice arose among
    The bleak twigs overhead
In a full-hearted evensong
    Of joy illimited ;

An aged thrush, frail, gaunt, and small,
    In blast-beruffled plume,
Had chosen thus to fling his soul
    Upon the growing gloom.

So little cause for carolings
    Of such ecstatic sound
Was written on terrestrial things
    Afar or nigh around,
That I could think there trembled through
    His happy good-night air
Some blessed Hope, whereof he knew
    And I was unaware.

*31st December* 1900.

# THE TEMPORARY THE ALL

## (SAPPHICS)

CHANGE and chancefulness in my flowering
    youthtime
Set me sun by sun near to one unchosen ;
Wrought us fellowlike, and despite divergence,
      Fused us in friendship.

" Cherish him can I while the true one forth-
    come—
Come the rich fulfiller of my prevision ;
Life is roomy yet, and the odds unbounded."
      So self-communed I.

'Thwart my wistful way did a damsel saunter,
Fair, albeit unformed to be all-eclipsing ;
" Maiden meet," held I, " till arise my forefelt
      Wonder of women."

Long a visioned hermitage deep desiring,
Tenements uncouth I was fain to house in :
" Let such lodging be for a breath-while,"
    thought I,
      " Soon a more seemly.

" Then high handiwork will I make my life-
    deed,
Truth and Light outshow ; but the ripe time
    pending,
Intermissive aim at the thing sufficeth."
       Thus I. . . . But lo, me !

Mistress, friend, place, aims to be bettered
    straightway,
Bettered not has Fate or my hand's achieve-
    ment ;
Sole the showance those of my onward earth-
    track—
       Never transcended !

# THE GHOST OF THE PAST

WE two kept house, the Past and I,
　　The Past and I ;
Through all my tasks it hovered nigh,
　　Leaving me never alone.
It was a spectral housekeeping
　　Where fell no jarring tone,
As strange, as still a housekeeping
　　As ever has been known.

As daily I went up the stair
　　And down the stair,
I did not mind the Bygone there—
　　The Present once to me ;
Its moving meek companionship
　　I wished might ever be,
There was in that companionship
　　Something of ecstasy.

It dwelt with me just as it was,
　　Just as it was
When first its prospects gave me pause
　　In wayward wanderings,

Before the years had torn old troths
　　As they tear all sweet things,
Before gaunt griefs had torn old troths
　　And dulled old rapturings.

And then its form began to fade,
　　　Began to fade,
Its gentle echoes faintlier played
　　At eves upon my ear
Than when the autumn's look embrowned
　　The lonely chambers here,
When autumn's settling shades embrowned
　　Nooks that it haunted near.

And so with time my vision less,
　　　Yea, less and less
Makes of that Past my housemistress,
　　It dwindles in my eye ;
It looms a far-off skeleton
　　And not a comrade nigh,
A fitful far-off skeleton
　　Dimming as days draw by.

## THE SELF-UNSEEING

HERE is the ancient floor,
Footworn and hollowed and thin,
Here was the former door
Where the dead feet walked in.

She sat here in her chair,
Smiling into the fire ;
He who played stood there,
Bowing it higher and higher.

Childlike, I danced in a dream ;
Blessings emblazoned that day ;
Everything glowed with a gleam ;
Yet we were looking away !

# TO LIFE

O LIFE with the sad seared face,
    I weary of seeing thee,
And thy draggled cloak, and thy hobbling pace,
    And thy too-forced pleasantry !

I know what thou would'st tell
    Of Death, Time, Destiny—
I have known it long, and know, too, well
    What it all means for me.

But canst thou not array
    Thyself in rare disguise,
And feign like truth, for one mad day,
    That Earth is Paradise ?

I'll tune me to the mood,
    And mumm with thee till eve
And maybe what as interlude
    I feign, I shall believe !

# UNKNOWING

WHEN, soul in soul reflected,
We breathed an æthered air,
    When we neglected
    All things elsewhere,
And left the friendly friendless
To keep our love aglow,
    We deemed it endless . . .
    —We did not know!

When panting passion-goaded,
We planned to hie away,
    But, unforeboded,
    All the long day
The storm so pierced and pattered
That none could up and go,
    Our lives seemed shattered . . .
    —We did not know!

When I found you helpless lying,
And you waived my long misprise,
    And swore me, dying,
    In phantom-guise

To wing to me when grieving,
And touch away my woe,
    We kissed, believing . . .
    —We did not know !

But though, your powers outreckoning,
You tarry dead and dumb,
    Or scorn my beckoning,
    And will not come :
And I say, " Why thus inanely
Brood on her memory so ! "
    I say it vainly—
    I feel and know !

# SHE AT HIS FUNERAL

THEY bear him to his resting-place—
In slow procession sweeping by ;
I follow at a stranger's space ;
His kindred they, his sweetheart I.
Unchanged my gown of garish dye,
Though sable-sad is their attire ;
But they stand round with griefless eye,
Whilst my regret consumes like fire !

187—.

# THE FIDDLER

THE fiddler knows what's brewing
 To the lilt of his lyric wiles :
The fiddler knows what rueing
 Will come of this night's smiles !

He sees couples join them for dancing,
 And afterwards joining for life,
He sees them pay high for their prancing
 By a welter of wedded strife.

He twangs : " Music hails from the devil,
 Though vaunted to come from heaven
For it makes people do at a revel
 What multiplies sins by seven.

" There's many a heart now mangled,
 And waiting its time to go,
Whose tendrils were first entangled
 By my sweet viol and bow ! "

# LOST LOVE

I PLAY my sweet old airs—
    The airs he knew
    When our love was true—
    But he does not balk
    His determined walk,
And passes up the stairs.

I sing my songs once more,
    And presently hear
    His footstep near
    As if it would stay ;
    But he goes his way,
And shuts a distant door.

So I wait for another morn,
    And another night
    In this soul-sick blight ;
    And I wonder much
    As I sit, why such
A woman as I was born !

# THE GOING

WHY did you give no hint that night
That quickly after the morrow's dawn,
And calmly, as if indifferent quite,
You would close your term here, up and be
      gone
      Where I could not follow
      With wing of swallow
To gain one glimpse of you ever anon !

      Never to bid good-bye,
      Or lip me the softest call,
Or utter a wish for a word, while I
Saw morning harden upon the wall,
      Unmoved, unknowing
      That your great going
Had place that moment, and altered all.

Why do you make me leave the house
And think for a breath it is you I see
At the end of the alley of bending boughs
Where so often at dusk you used to be ;
      Till in darkening dankness
      The yawning blankness
Of the perspective sickens me !

You were she who abode
By those red-veined rocks far West,
You were the swan-necked one who rode
Along the beetling Beeny Crest,
And, reining nigh me,
Would muse and eye me,
While Life unrolled us its very best.

Why, then, latterly did we not speak,
Did we not think of those days long dead,
And ere your vanishing strive to seek
That time's renewal ? We might have said,
" In this bright spring weather
We'll visit together
Those places that once we visited."

Well, well ! All's past amend,
Unchangeable. It must go.
I seem but a dead man held on end
To sink down soon. . . . O you could **not** know
That such swift fleeing
No soul foreseeing—
Not even I—would undo me so !

*December* 1912.

## " I FOUND HER OUT THERE "

I FOUND her out there
On a slope few see.
That falls westwardly
To the salt-edged air,
Where the ocean breaks
On the purple strand,
And the hurricane shakes
The solid land.

I brought her here,
And have laid her to rest
In a noiseless nest
No sea beats near.
She will never be stirred
In her loamy cell
By the waves long heard
And loved so well.

So she does not sleep
By those haunted heights
The Atlantic smites
And the blind gales sweep,

Whence she often would gaze
At Dundagel's famed head,
While the dipping blaze
Dyed her face fire-red ;

And would sigh at the tale
Of sunk Lyonnesse,
As a wind-tugged tress
Flapped her cheek like a flail;
Or listen at whiles
With a thought-bound brow
To the murmuring miles
She is far from now.

Yet her shade, maybe,
Will creep underground
Till it catch the sound
Of that western sea
As it swells and sobs
Where she once domiciled,
And joy in its throbs
With the heart of a child.

# THE VOICE

WOMAN much missed, how you call to me, call
      to me,
Saying that now you are not as you were
When you had changed from the one who was
      all to me,
But as at first, when our day was fair.

Can it be you that I hear ?   Let me view you,
      then,
Standing as when I drew near to the town
Where you would wait for me : yes, as I knew
      you then,
Even to the original air-blue gown !

Or is it only the breeze, in its listlessness
Travelling across the wet mead to me here,
You being ever dissolved to wan wistlessness,
Heard no more again far or near ?

    Thus I ;  faltering forward,
    Leaves around me falling,
Wind  oozing  thin  through  the  thorn  from
      norward,
    And the woman calling.

*December* 1912.

# AFTER A JOURNEY

HERETO I come to view a voiceless ghost;
   Whither, O whither will its whim now draw
        me ?
Up the cliff, down, till I'm lonely, lost,
   And the unseen waters' ejaculations awe me.
Where you will next be there's no knowing,
   Facing round about me everywhere,
       With your nut-coloured hair,
And gray eyes, and rose-flush coming and
    going.

Yes: I have re-entered your olden haunts at
    last ;
   Through the years, through the dead scenes
     I have tracked you ;
What have you now found to say of our past—
   Scanned across the dark space wherein I have
     lacked you ?
Summer gave us sweets, but autumn wrought
    division ?
   Things were not lastly as firstly well
     With us twain, you tell ?
But all's closed now, despite Time's derision.

I see what you are doing : you are leading
    me on
    To the spots we knew when we haunted here
      together,
The waterfall, above which the mist-bow shone
    At the then fair hour in the then fair weather,
And the cave just under, with a voice still so
    hollow
    That it seems to call out to me from forty
      years ago,
      When you were all aglow,
And not the thin ghost that I now frailly follow !

Ignorant of what there is flitting here to see,
    The waked birds preen and the seals flop
      lazily,
Soon you will have, Dear, to vanish from me,
    For the stars close their shutters and the
      dawn whitens hazily.
Trust me, I mind not, though Life lours,
    The bringing me here ; nay, bring me here
      again !
      I am just the same as when
Our days were a joy, and our paths through
    flowers.

PENTARGAN BAY.

# BEENY CLIFF

*March* 1870—*March* 1913

## I

O THE opal and the sapphire of that wandering
  western sea,
And the woman riding high above with bright
  hair flapping free—
The woman whom I loved so, and who loyally
  loved me.

## II

The pale mews plained below us, and the waves
  seemed far away
In a nether sky, engrossed in saying their cease-
  less babbling say,
As we laughed light-heartedly aloft on that clear-
  sunned March day.

## III

A little cloud then cloaked us, and there flew an
  irised rain,
And the Atlantic dyed its levels with a dull mis-
  featured stain,
And then the sun burst out again, and purples
  prinked the main.

### IV

—Still in all its chasmal beauty bulks old Beeny
    to the sky,
And shall she and I not go there once again now
    March is nigh,
And the sweet things said in that March say
    anew there by and by ?

### V

What if still in chasmal beauty looms that wild
    weird western shore,
The woman now is—elsewhere—whom the
    ambling pony bore,
And nor knows nor cares for Beeny, and will
    laugh there nevermore.

## AT CASTLE BOTEREL

As I drive to the junction of lane and highway,
 And the drizzle bedrenches the waggonette,
I look behind at the fading byway,
 And see on its slope, now glistening wet,
  Distinctly yet

Myself and a girlish form benighted
 In dry March weather. We climb the road
Beside a chaise. We had just alighted
 To ease the sturdy pony's load
  When he sighed and slowed.

What we did as we climbed, and what we
  talked of
 Matters not much, nor to what it led,—
Something that life will not be balked of
 Without rude reason till hope is dead,
  And feeling fled.

It filled but a minute. But was there ever
 A time of such quality, since or before,
In that hill's story ? To one mind never,
 Though it has been climbed, foot-swift, foot-
  sore,
  By thousands more.

Primaeval rocks form the road's steep border,
  And much have they faced there, first and
      last,
Of the transitory in Earth's long order ;
  But what they record in colour and cast
      Is—that we two passed.

And to me, though Time's unflinching rigour,
  In mindless rote, has ruled from sight
The substance now, one phantom figure
  Remains on the slope, as when that night
      Saw us alight.

I look and see it there, shrinking, shrinking,
  I look back at it amid the rain
For the very last time ; for my sand is sinking,
  And I shall traverse old love's domain
      Never again.

    *March* 1913.

# THE PHANTOM HORSEWOMAN

### I

QUEER are the ways of a man I know :
         He comes and stands
         In a careworn craze,
         And looks at the sands
         And the seaward haze
         With moveless hands
         And face and gaze,
         Then turns to go . . .
And what does he see when he gazes so ?

### II

They say he sees as an instant thing
         More clear than to-day,
         A sweet soft scene
         That was once in play
         By that briny green ;
         Yes, notes alway
         Warm, real, and keen,
         What his back years bring—
A phantom of his own figuring.

66

### III

Of this vision of his they might say more :
   Not only there
   Does he see this sight,
   But everywhere
   In his brain—day, night,
   As if on the air
   It were drawn rose-bright—
   Yea, far from that shore
Does he carry this vision of heretofore :

### IV

A ghost-girl-rider.   And though, toil-tried
   He withers daily,
   Time touches her not,
   But she still rides gaily
   In his rapt thought
   On that shagged and shaly
   Atlantic spot,
   And as when first eyed
Draws rein and sings to the swing of the tide.

**1913**

# WHERE THE PICNIC WAS

WHERE we made the fire
In the summer time
Of branch and briar
On the hill to the sea.
I slowly climb
Through winter mire,
And scan and trace
The forsaken place
Quite readily.

Now a cold wind blows,
And the grass is gray,
But the spot still shows
As a burnt circle—aye,
And stick-ends, charred,
Still strew the sward
Whereon I stand,
Last relic of the band
Who came that day !

Yes, I am here
Just as last year,

And the sea breathes brine
From its strange straight line
Up hither, the same
As when we four came.
—But two have wandered far
From this grassy rise
Into urban roar
Where no picnics are,
And one—has shut her eyes
For evermore.

# ON A MIDSUMMER EVE

I IDLY cut a parsley stalk,
And blew therein towards the moon ;
I had not thought what ghosts would walk
With shivering footsteps to my tune.

I went, and knelt, and scooped my hand
As if to drink, into the brook,
And a faint figure seemed to stand
Above me, with the bygone look.

I lipped rough rhymes of chance, not choice,
I thought not what my words might be ;
There came into my ear a voice
That turned a tenderer verse for me.

# " MY SPIRIT WILL NOT HAUNT THE MOUND "

My spirit will not haunt the mound
    Above my breast,
But travel, memory-possessed,
To where my tremulous being found
    Life largest, best.

My phantom-footed shape will go
    When nightfall grays
Hither and thither along the ways
I and another used to know
    In backward days.

And there you'll find me, if a jot
    You still should care
For me, and for my curious air;
If otherwise, then I shall not,
    For you, be there.

# THE HOUSE OF HOSPITALITIES

HERE we broached the Christmas barrel,
　　Pushed up the charred log-ends ;
Here we sang the Christmas carol,
　　And called in friends.

Time has tired me since we met here
　　When the folk now dead were young,
Since the viands were outset here
　　And quaint songs sung.

And the worm has bored the viol
　　That used to lead the tune,
Rust eaten out the dial
　　That struck night's noon.

Now no Christmas brings in neighbours,
　　And the New Year comes unlit ;
Where we sang the mole now labours,
　　And spiders knit.

Yet at midnight if here walking,
　　When the moon sheets wall and tree,
I see forms of old time talking,
　　Who smile on me.

# SHUT OUT THAT MOON

CLOSE up the casement, draw the blind,
    Shut out that stealing moon,
She wears too much the guise she wore
    Before our lutes were strewn
With years-deep dust, and names we read
    On a white stone were hewn.

Step not forth on the dew-dashed lawn
    To view the Lady's Chair,
Immense Orion's glittering form,
    The Less and Greater Bear:
Stay in; to such sights we were drawn
    When faded ones were fair.

Brush not the bough for midnight scents
    That come forth lingeringly,
And wake the same sweet sentiments
    They breathed to you and me
When living seemed a laugh, and love
    All it was said to be.

Within the common lamp-lit room
    Prison my eyes and thought;
Let dingy details crudely loom,
    Mechanic speech be wrought:
Too fragrant was Life's early bloom
    Too tart the fruit it brought!

1904.

## " REGRET NOT ME "

Regret not me ;
Beneath the sunny tree
I lie uncaring, slumbering peacefully

Swift as the light
I flew my faery flight ;
Ecstatically I moved, and feared no night.

I did not know
That heydays fade and go,
But deemed that what was would be always so

I skipped at morn
Between the yellowing corn,
Thinking it good and glorious to be born.

I ran at eves
Among the piled-up sheaves,
Dreaming, " I grieve not, therefore nothing
grieves."

Now soon will come
The apple pear, and plum,
And hinds will sing, and autumn insects hum.

74

Again you will fare
To cider-makings rare,
And junketings ; but I shall not be there.

Yet gaily sing
Until the pewter ring
Those songs we sang when we went gipsying.

And lightly dance
Some triple-timed romance
In coupled figures, and forget mischance ;

And mourn not me
Beneath the yellowing tree ;
For I shall mind not, slumbering peacefully.

# IN THE MIND'S EYE

That was once her casement,
    And the taper nigh,
Shining from within there,
    Beckoned, " Here am I ! "

Now, as then, I see her
    Moving at the pane ;
Ah ; 'tis but her phantom
    Borne within my brain !—

Foremost in my vision
    Everywhere goes she ;
Change dissolves the landscapes,
    She abides with me.

Shape so sweet and shy, Dear,
    Who can say thee nay ?
Never once do I, Dear,
    Wish thy ghost away.

# AMABEL

I MARKED her ruined hues,
Her custom-straitened views,
And asked, " Can there indwell
    My Amabel ? "

I looked upon her gown,
Once rose, now earthen brown ;
The change was like the knell
    Of Amabel.

Her step's mechanic ways
Had lost the life of May's ;
Her laugh, once sweet in swell,
    Spoilt Amabel.

I mused : " Who sings the strain
I sang ere warmth did wane ?
Who thinks its numbers spell
    His Amabel ? "—

Knowing that, though Love cease,
Love's race shows no decrease ;
All find in dorp or dell
    An Amabel.

—I felt that I could creep
To some housetop, and weep
That Time the tyrant fell
     Ruled Amabel !

I said (the while I sighed
That love like ours had died),
" Fond things I'll no more tell
     To Amabel,

" But leave her to her fate,
And fling across the gate,
' Till the Last Trump, farewell,
     O Amabel ! ' "

     1865.

## " I SAID TO LOVE "

I SAID to Love,
" It is not now as in old days
When men adored thee and thy ways
      All else above ;
Named thee the Boy, the Bright, the One
Who spread a heaven beneath the sun,"
      I said to Love.

I said to him,
" We now know more of thee than then ;
We were but weak in judgment when,
      With hearts abrim,
We clamoured thee that thou would'st please
Inflict on us thine agonies,"
      I said to him.

I said to Love,
" Thou art not young, thou art not fair,
No elfin darts, no cherub air,
      Nor swan, nor dove
Are thine ;  but features pitiless,
And iron daggers of distress,"
      I said to Love.

79

"Depart then, Love ! . . .
—Man's race shall perish, threatenest thou,
Without thy kindling coupling-vow ?
The age to come the man of now
          Know nothing of ?—
We fear not such a threat from thee ;
We are too old in apathy !
*Mankind shall cease.*—So let it be,"
          I said to Love.

# REMINISCENCES OF A DANCING MAN

## I

WHO now remembers Almack's balls—
    Willis's sometime named—
In those two smooth-floored upper halls
    For faded ones so famed?
Where as we trod to trilling sound
The fancied phantoms stood around,
    Or joined us in the maze,
Of the powdered Dears from Georgian years,
Whose dust lay in sightless sealed-up biers,
    The fairest of former days.

## II

Who now remembers gay Cremorne,
    And all its jaunty jills,
And those wild whirling figures born
    Of Jullien's grand quadrilles?
With hats on head and morning coats
There footed to his prancing notes
    Our partner-girls and we;
And the gas-jets winked, and the lustres clinked,
And the platform throbbed as with arms en-
    linked
    We moved to the minstrelsy.

### III

Who now recalls those crowded rooms
    Of old yclept " The Argyle,"
Where to the deep Drum-polka's booms
    We hopped in standard style ?
Whither have danced those damsels now !
Is Death the partner who doth moue
    Their wormy chaps and bare ?
Do their spectres spin like sparks within
The smoky halls of the Prince of Sin
    To a thunderous Jullien air ?

# IN A WOOD

PALE beech and pine so blue,
 Set in one clay,
Bough to bough cannot you
 Live out your day ?
When the rains skim and skip,
Why mar sweet comradeship,
Blighting with poison-drip
 Neighbourly spray ?

Heart-halt and spirit-lame,
 City-opprest,
Unto this wood I came
 As to a nest ,
Dreaming that sylvan peace
Offered the harrowed ease—
Nature a soft release
 From men's unrest.

But, having entered in,
 Great growths and small.
Show them to men akin—·
 Combatants all !

Sycamore shoulders oak,
Bines the slim sapling yoke,
Ivy-spun halters choke
    Elms stout and tall.

Touches from ash, O wych,
    Sting you like scorn !
You, too, brave hollies, twitch
    Sidelong from thorn.
Even the rank poplars bear
Lothly a rival's air,
Cankering in blank despair
    If overborne.

Since, then, no grace I find
    Taught me of trees,
Turn I back to my kind,
    Worthy as these.
There at least smiles abound,
There discourse trills around,
There, now and then, are found
    Life-loyalties.

    1887 : 1896.

# HE ABJURES LOVE

At last I put off love,
  For twice ten years
The daysman of my thought,
  And hope, and doing ;
Being ashamed thereof,
  And faint of fears
And desolations, wrought
  In his pursuing,

Since first in youthtime those
  Disquietings
That heart-enslavement brings
  To hale and hoary,
Became my housefellows,
  And, fool and blind,
I turned from kith and kind
  To give him glory.

I was as children be
  Who have no care ;
I did not shrink or sigh,
  I did not sicken ;
But lo, Love beckoned me,
  And I was bare,

And poor, and starved, and dry,
   And fever-stricken.

Too many times ablaze
   With fatuous fires,
Enkindled by his wiles
   To new embraces,
Did I, by wilful ways
   And baseless ires,
Return the anxious smiles
   Of friendly faces.

No more will now rate I
   The common rare,
The midnight drizzle dew,
   The gray hour golden,
The wind a yearning cry.
   The faulty fair,
Things dreamt, of comelier hue
   Than things beholden ! . . .

—I speak as one who plumbs
   Life's dim profound,
One who at length can sound
   Clear views and certain.
But—after love what comes ?
   A scene that lours,
A few sad vacant hours,
   And then, the Curtain.

      1883.

# THE DREAM-FOLLOWER

A DREAM of mine flew over the mead
    To the halls where my old Love reigns ;
And it drew me on to follow its lead :
    And I stood at her window-panes ;

And I saw but a thing of flesh and bone
    Speeding on to its cleft in the clay ;
And my dream was scared, and expired on a
    moan,
    And I whitely hastened away.

# WESSEX HEIGHTS

## (1896)

THERE are some heights in Wessex, shaped as
    if by a kindly hand
For thinking, dreaming, dying on, and at crises
    when I stand,
Say, on Ingpen Beacon eastward, or on Wylls-
    Neck westwardly,
I seem where I was before my birth, and after
    death may be.

In the lowlands I have no comrade, not even
    the lone man's friend—
Her who suffereth long and is kind ; accepts
    what he is too weak to mend :
Down there they are dubious and askance ;
    there nobody thinks as I,
But mind-chains do not clank where one's next
    neighbour is the sky.

In the towns I am tracked by phantoms having
    weird detective ways—
Shadows of beings who fellowed with myself
    of earlier days :

88

They hang about at places, and they say harsh
    heavy things—
Men with a wintry sneer, and women with tart
    disparagings.


Down there I seem to be false to myself, my
    simple self that was,
And is not now, and I see him watching,
    wondering what crass cause
Can have merged him into such a strange
    continuator as this,
Who yet has something in common with him-
    self, my chrysalis.


I cannot go to the great **grey** Plain ; there's a
    figure against the moon,
Nobody sees it but I, and it makes my breast
    beat out of tune ;
I cannot go to the tall-spired town, being barred
    by the forms now passed
For everybody but me, in whose long vision
    they stand there fast.


There's a ghost at Yell'ham Bottom chiding
    loud at the fall of the night,
There's a ghost in Froom-side Vale, thin-lipped
    and vague, in a shroud of white,
There is one in the railway-train whenever I do
    not want it near,
I see its profile against the pane, saying what I
    would not hear.

As for one rare fair woman, I am now but a
    thought of hers,
I enter her mind and another thought succeeds
    me that she prefers ;
Yet my love for her in its fulness she herself
    even did not know ;
Well, time cures hearts of tenderness, and now
    I can let her go.

So I am found on Ingpen Beacon, or on Wylls-
    Neck to the west,
Or else on homely Bulbarrow, or little Pilsdon
    Crest,
Where men have never cared to haunt, nor
    women have walked with me,
And ghosts then keep their distance ; and I
    know some liberty.

# TO A MOTHERLESS CHILD

Ah, child, thou art but half thy darling mother's:
    Hers couldst thou wholly be,
My light in thee would outglow all in others;
    She would relive to me.
But niggard Nature's trick of birth
    Bars, lest she overjoy,
Renewal of the loved on earth
    Save with alloy.

The Dame has no regard, alas, my maiden,
    For love and loss like mine—
No sympathy with mindsight memory-laden;
    Only with fickle eyne.
To her mechanic artistry
    My dreams are all unknown,
And why I wish that thou couldst be
    But One's alone!

## " I NEED NOT GO "

I NEED not go
Through sleet and snow
To where I know
She waits for me ;
She will tarry me there
Till I find it fair,
And have time to spare
From company.

When I've overgot
The world somewhat,
When things cost not
Such stress and strain,
Is soon enough
By cypress sough
To tell my Love
I am come again.

And if some day,
When none cries nay,
I still delay
To seek her side,

(Though ample measure
Of fitting leisure
Await my pleasure)
She will not chide.

What—not upbraid me
That I delayed me,
Nor ask what stayed me
So long ?   Ah, no !—
New cares may claim me.
New loves inflame me,
She will not blame me,
But suffer it so.

# SHELLEY'S SKYLARK

*(The neighbourhood of Leghorn: March* 1887)

SOMEWHERE afield here something lies
In Earth's oblivious eyeless trust
That moved a poet to prophecies—
A pinch of unseen, unguarded dust :

The dust of the lark that Shelley heard,
And made immortal through times to be ;—
Though it only lived like another bird,
And knew not its immortality :

Lived its meek life ; then, one day, fell—
A little ball of feather and bone ;
And how it perished, when piped farewell,
And where it wastes, are alike unknown.

Maybe it rests in the loam I view,
Maybe it throbs in a myrtle's green,
Maybe it sleeps in the coming hue
Of a grape on the slopes of yon inland scene.

Go find it, faeries, go and find
That tiny pinch of priceless dust,

And bring a casket silver-lined,
And framed of gold that gems encrust ;

And we will lay it safe therein,
And consecrate it to endless time ;
For it inspired a bard to win
Ecstatic heights in thought and rhyme.

# WIVES IN THE SERE

## I

Never a careworn wife but shows,
　　If a joy suffuse her,
Something beautiful to those
　　Patient to peruse her,
Some one charm the world unknows,
　　Precious to a muser,
Haply what, ere years were foes,
　　Moved her mate to choose her.

## II

But, be it a hint of rose
　　That an instant hues her,
Or some early light or pose
　　Wherewith thought renews her—
Seen by him at full, ere woes
　　Practised to abuse her—
Sparely comes it, swiftly goes,
　　Time again subdues her.

# WEATHERS

## I

THIS is the weather the cuckoo likes,
    And so do I ;
When showers betumble the chestnut spikes,
    And nestlings fly :
And the little brown nightingale bills his best,
And they sit outside at " The Travellers' Rest,"
And maids come forth sprig-muslin drest,
And citizens dream of the south and west,
    And so do I.

## II

This is the weather the shepherd shuns,
    And so do I ;
When beeches drip in browns and duns,
    And thresh, and ply ;
And hill-hid tides throb, throe on throe,
And meadow rivulets overflow,
And drops on gate-bars hang in a row,
And rooks in families homeward go,
    And so do I.

# EPEISODIA

## I

PAST the hills that peep
Where the leaze is smiling,
On and on beguiling
Crisply-cropping sheep ;
Under boughs of brushwood
Linking tree and tree
In a shade of lushwood,
    There caressed we !

## II

Hemmed by city walls
That outshut the sunlight,
In a foggy dun light,
Where the footstep falls
With a pit-pat wearisome
In its cadency
On the flagstones drearisome
    There pressed we !

III

Where in wild-winged crowds
Blown birds show their whiteness
Up against the lightness
Of the clammy clouds ;
By the random river
Pushing to the sea,
Under bents that quiver
    There shall rest we.

# JOYS OF MEMORY

WHEN the spring comes round, and a certain
        day
Looks out from the brume by the eastern
        copsetrees
        And says, Remember,
    I begin again, as if it were new,
    A day of like date I once lived through,
    Whiling it hour by hour away ;
        So shall I do till my December,
          When spring comes round.

    I take my holiday then and my rest
Away from the dun life here about me,
        Old hours re-greeting
    With the quiet sense that bring they must
    Such throbs as at first, till I house with dust,
    And in the numbness my heartsome zest
        For things that were, be past repeating
        When spring comes round.

# TO THE MOON

" WHAT have you looked at, Moon,
    In your time,
  Now long past your prime ? "
" O, I have looked at, often looked at
    Sweet, sublime,
Sore things, shudderful, night and noon
    In my time."

  " What have you mused on, Moon,
    In your day,
  So aloof, so far away ? "
" O, I have mused on, often mused on
    Growth, decay,
Nations alive, dead, mad, aswoon,
    In my day ! "

  " Have you much wondered, Moon,
    On your rounds,
  Self-wrapt, beyond Earth's bounds ? "
" Yea, I have wondered, often wondered
    At the sounds
Reaching me of the human tune
    On my rounds."

" What do you think of it, Moon,
　　As you go ?
　Is Life much, or no ? "
" O, I think of it, often think of it
　　As a show
God ought surely to shut up soon,
　　As I go."

# TIMING HER

*(Written to an old folk-tune)*

LALAGE'S coming :
Where is she now, O ?
Turning to bow, O,
And smile, is she,
Just at parting,
Parting, parting,
As she is starting
To come to me ?

Where is she now, O,
Now, and now, O,
Shadowing a bough, O,
Of hedge or tree
As she is rushing,
Rushing, rushing,
Gossamers brushing
To come to me ?

Lalage's coming ;
Where is she now, O ;
Climbing the brow, O,
Of hills I see ?

Yes, she is nearing,
Nearing, nearing,
Weather unfearing
To come to me.

Near is she now, O,
Now, and now, O ;
Milk the rich cow, O,
Forward the tea ;
Shake the down bed for her,
Linen sheets spread for her,
Drape round the head for her
Coming to me.

Lalage's coming,
She's nearer now, O,
End anyhow, O,
To-day's husbandry !
Would a gilt chair were mine,
Slippers of vair were mine,
Brushes for hair were mine
Of ivory !

What will she think, O,
She who's so comely,
Viewing how homely
A sort are we !
Nothing resplendent,
No prompt attendant,
Not one dependent
Pertaining to me !

Lalage's coming ;
Where is she now, O ?
Fain I'd avow, O,
Full honestly
Nought here's enough for her,
All is too rough for her,
Even my love for her
Poor in degree.

She's nearer now, O,
Still nearer now, O,
She 'tis, I vow, O,
Passing the lea.
Rush down to meet her there,
Call out and greet her there,
Never a sweeter there
Crossed to me !

Lalage's come ; aye,
Come is she now, O ! . . .
Does Heaven allow, O,
A meeting to be ?
Yes, she is here now,
Here now, here now,
Nothing to fear now,
Here's Lalage !

# "THE CURTAINS NOW ARE DRAWN"

## (SONG)

### I

THE curtains now are drawn,
And the spindrift strikes the glass,
Blown up the jaggèd pass
By the surly salt sou'-west,
And the sneering glare is gone
Behind the yonder crest,
    While she sings to me :
"O the dream that thou art my Love, be it
        thine,
And the dream that I am thy Love, be it mine,
And death may come, but loving is divine."

### II

I stand here in the rain,
With its smite upon her stone,
And the grasses that have grown
Over women, children, men,
And their texts that " Life is vain ; "

But I hear the notes as when
    Once she sang to me :
" O  the  dream  that  thou  art  my  Love,  be  it
      thine,
And the dream that I am thy Love, be it mine,
And death may come, but loving is divine."

    1913.

# " AS 'TWERE TO-NIGHT "

## (SONG)

As 'twere to-night, in the brief space
      Of a far eventime,
      My spirit rang achime
At vision of a girl of grace ;
As 'twere to-night, in the brief space
      Of a far eventime.

As 'twere at noontide of to-morrow
      I airily walked and talked,
      And wondered as I walked
What it could mean, this soar from sorrow ;
As 'twere at noontide of to-morrow
      I airily walked and talked.

As 'twere at waning of this week
      Broke a new life on me ;
      Trancings of bliss to be
In some dim dear land soon to seek ;
As 'twere at waning of this week
      Broke a new life on me !

# SAYING GOOD-BYE

## (SONG)

WE are always saying
    " Good-bye, good-bye ! "
In work, in playing,
In gloom, in gaying :
    At many a stage
    Of pilgrimage
    From youth to age
    We say, " Good-bye,
        Good-bye ! "

We are undiscerning
    Which go to sigh,
Which will be yearning
For soon returning ;
    And which no more
    Will dark our door
    Or tread our shore
    But go to die,
        To die.

Some come from roaming
      With joy again ;
Some, who come homing
By stealth at gloaming,
      Had better have stopped
      Till death, and dropped
      By strange hands propped,
      Than come so fain,
            So fain.

So, with this saying,
      " Good-bye, good-bye,"
We speed their waying
Without betraying
      Our grief, our fear
      No more to hear
      From them, close, clear,
      Again : " Good-bye,
            Good-bye ! "

## "ANY LITTLE OLD SONG"

Any little old song
   Will do for me,
Tell it of joys gone long,
   Or joys to be,
Or friendly faces best
   Loved to see.

Newest themes I want not
   On subtle strings,
And for thrillings pant not
   That new song brings :
I only need the homeliest
   Of heartstirrings.

# LOVER TO MISTRESS

## (SONG)

BECKON to me to come
With handkerchief or hand,
Or finger mere or thumb ;
Let forecasts be but rough,
Parents more bleak than bland,
    'Twill be enough,
        Maid mine,
    'Twill be enough !

Two fields, a wood, a tree,
Nothing now more malign
Lies between you and me ;
But were they bysm, or bluff,
Or snarling sea, one sign ,
    Would be enough,
        Maid mine,
    Would be enough !

From an old copy.

# COME NOT ; YET COME !

## (SONG)

IN my sage moments I can say,
    Come not near,
But far in foreign regions stay,
    So that here
A mind may grow again serene and clear.

But the thought withers.   Why should I
    Have fear to earn me
Fame from your nearness, though thereby
    Old fires new burn me,
And lastly, maybe, tear and overturn me !

So I say, Come : deign again shine
    Upon this place,
Even if unslackened smart be mine
    From that sweet face,
And I faint to a phantom past all trace.

## " LET ME BELIEVE "

### (SONG)

LET me believe it, dearest,
     Let it be
As just a dream—-the merest—
     Haunting me,
That a frank full-souled sweetness
     Warmed your smile
And voice, to indiscreetness
     Once, awhile !

And I will fondly ponder
     Till I lie
Earthed up with others yonder
     Past a sigh,
That you may name at stray times
     With regret
One whom through green and gray times
     You forget !

# LAST LOVE-WORD

## (SONG)

THIS is the last ; the very, very last !
   Anon, and all is dead and dumb,
   Only a pale shroud over the past,
     That cannot be
     Of value small or vast,
      Love, then to me !

I can say no more :  I have even said too much.
   I did not mean that this should come :
   I did not know 'twould swell to such—
     Nor, perhaps, you—
     When that first look and touch,
      Love, doomed us two !

189–.

# SINGING LOVERS

I ROWED : the dimpled tide was at the turn,
And mirth and moonlight spread upon the
        bay :
There were two singing lovers in the stern ;
        But mine had gone away,—
        Whither, I shunned to say !


The houses stood confronting us afar,
A livid line against the evening glare ;
The small lamps livened ; then out-stole a
        star ;
        But my Love was not there,—
        Vanished, I sorrowed where !


His arm was round her, both full facing me
With no reserve. Theirs was not love to
        hide ;
He held one tiller-rope, the other she ;
        I pulled—the merest glide,—
        Looked on at them, and sighed.

The moon's glassed glory heaved as we lay
      swinging
Upon the undulations.   Shoreward, slow,
The plash of pebbles joined the lovers' singing,
      But she of a bygone vow
      Joined in the song not now !

WEYMOUTH.

## " SOMETHING  TAPPED "

Something tapped on the pane of my room
   When there was never a trace
Of wind or rain, and I saw in the gloom
   My weary Belovéd's face.

" O I am tired of waiting," she said,
   " Night, morn, noon, afternoon ;
So cold it is in my lonely bed,
   And I thought you would join me soon ! "

I rose and neared the window-glass,
   But vanished thence had she :
Only a pallid moth, alas,
   Tapped at the pane for me.

   *August* 1913.

# GREAT THINGS

SWEET cyder is a great thing,
  A great thing to me,
Spinning down to Weymouth town
  By Ridgway thirstily,
And maid and mistress summoning
  Who tend the hostelry :
O cyder is a great thing,
  A great thing to me !

The dance it is a great thing,
  A great thing to me,
With candles lit and partners fit
  For night-long revelry ;
And going home when day-dawning
  Peeps pale upon the lea :
O dancing is a great thing,
  A great thing to me !

Love is, yea, a great thing,
  A great thing to me,
When, having drawn across the lawn
  In darkness silently,
A figure flits like one a-wing
  Out from the nearest tree :
O love is, yes, a great thing,
  A great thing to me !

119

Will these be always great things,
  Great things to me ? . . .
Let it befall that One will call,
  " Soul, I have need of thee : "
What then ?   Joy-jaunts, impassioned flings,
  Love, and its ecstasy,
Will always have been great things,
  Great things to me !

# THE SINGING WOMAN

THERE was a singing woman
   Came riding across the mead
At the time of the mild May weather,
     Tameless, tireless ;
This song she sung: " I am fair, I am young ! "
   And many turned to heed.

And the same singing woman
   Sat crooning in her need
At the time of the winter weather ;
     Friendless, fireless,
She sang this song : " Life, thou'rt too long ! "
   And there was none to heed.

# THE LAST TIME

THE kiss had been given and taken,
    And gathered to many past :
It never could reawaken ;
    But I heard none say : " It's the last ! "

The clock showed the hour and the minute
    But I did not turn and look :
I read no finis in it,
    As at closing of a book.

But I read it all too rightly
    When, at a time anon,
A figure lay stretched out whitely,
    And I stood looking thereon.

# TWO LIPS

I KISSED them in fancy as I came
    Away in the morning glow :
I kissed them through the glass of her picture·
    frame :
        She did not know.

I kissed them in love, in troth, in laughter,
    When she knew all ; long so !
That I should kiss them in a shroud thereafter
    She did not know.

# JUST THE SAME

I SAT.   It all was past ;
Hope never would hail again ;
Fair days had ceased at a blast,
The world was a darkened den.

The beauty and dream were gone,
And the halo in which I had hied
So gaily gallantly on
Had suffered blot and died !

I went forth, heedless whither,
In a cloud too black for name :
—People frisked hither and thither ;
The world was just the same.

# THE BLINDED BIRD

So zestfully canst thou sing ?
And all this indignity,
With God's consent, on thee !
Blinded ere yet a-wing
By the red-hot needle thou,
I stand and wonder how
So zestfully thou canst sing !

Resenting not such wrong,
Thy grievous pain forgot,
Eternal dark thy lot,
Groping thy whole life long,
After that stab of fire ;
Enjailed in pitiless wire ;
Resenting not such wrong !

Who hath charity ?   This bird.
Who suffereth long and is kind,
Is not provoked, though blind
And alive ensepulchred ?
Who hopeth, endureth all things ?
Who thinketh no evil, but sings ?
Who is divine ?   This bird.

# THE CHIMES PLAY " LIFE'S A BUMPER ! "

" Awake !    I'm off to cities far away,"
I said ; and rose. on peradventures bent.
The chimes played " Life's a Bumper ! " long
    that day
To the measure of my walking as I went :
Their sweetness frisked and floated on the lea,
As they played out " Life's a Bumper ! " there
    to me.

" Awake ! " I said.    " I go to take a bride ! "
—The sun arose behind me ruby-red
As I journeyed townwards from the countryside,
The chiming bells saluting near ahead.
Their sweetness swelled in tripping tings of glee
As they played out " Life's a Bumper ! " there
    to me.

" Again arise."    I seek a turfy slope,
And go forth slowly on an autumn noon,
And there I lay her who has been my hope,
And think, " O may I follow hither soon ! "
While on the wind the. chimes come cheerily,
Playing out " Life's a Bumper ! " there to me.

1913.

# THE MONUMENT-MAKER

I CHISELLED her monument
    To my mind's content,
Took it to the church by night,
When her planet was at its height,
And set it where I had figured the place in the
        daytime.
    Having niched it there
I stepped back, cheered, and thought its out-
    lines fair,
    And its marbles rare.


Then laughed she over my shoulder as in our
        Maytime :
    " It spells not me ! " she said :
" Tells nothing about my beauty, wit, or gay
        time
    With all those, quick and dead,
    Of high or lowlihead,
        That hovered near,
Including you, who carve there your devotion ;
    But you felt none, my dear ! "

127

And  then  she  vanished.    Checkless sprang my
          emotion,
        And forced a tear
At seeing I'd not been truly known by her,
And never prized !—that my memorial here,
    To consecrate her sepulchre,
        Was scorned, almost,
        By her sweet ghost :
Yet I hoped not quite, in her very innermost '

    1916.

# "COULD HE BUT LIVE FOR ME"

*(Iseult's Song: Queen of Cornwall)*

COULD he but live for me
A day, yea, even an hour,
Its petty span would be
Steeped in felicity
Passing the price of Heaven's held-dearest
dower :
Could he but live, could *he*
But live for me !

Could he but come to me
Amid these murks that lour,
My hollow life would be
So brimmed with ecstasy
As heart-dry honeysuck by summer shower :
Could he but come, could he
But come to me !

129

# "LET'S MEET AGAIN TO-NIGHT, MY FAIR"

### (*Tristram's Song: Queen of Cornwall*)

LET's meet again to-night, my Fair,
  Let's meet unseen of all ;
The day-god labours to his lair,
  And then the evenfall !

O living lute, O lily-rose,
  O form of fantasie,
When torches waste and warders doze
  Steal to the stars will we !

While nodding knights carouse at meat
  And shepherds shamble home,
We'll cleave in close embracements—sweet
  As honey in the comb !

Till crawls the dawn from Condol's crown,
  And over Neitan's Kieve,
As grimly ghosts we conjure down
  And hopes still weave and weave !

# SONG TO AN OLD BURDEN

THE feet have left the wormholed flooring,
    That danced to the ancient air,
    The fiddler, all-ignoring,
Sleeps by the gray-grassed 'cello player :
Shall I then foot around around around,
    As once I footed there !

The voice is heard in the room no longer
    That trilled, none sweetlier,
    To gentle stops or stronger,
Where now the dust-draped cobwebs stir :
Shall I then sing again again again,
    As once I sang with her !

The eyes that beamed out rapid brightness
    Have longtime found their close,
    The cheeks have wanned to whiteness
That used to sort with summer rose :
Shall I then joy anew anew anew,
    As once I joyed in those !

O what's to me this tedious Maying,
    What's to me this June ?
    O why should viols be playing
To catch and reel and rigadoon ?
Shall I sing, dance around around around,
    When phantoms call the tune !

## " WHY DO I ? "

Why do I go on doing these things ?
        Why not cease ?—
Is it that you are yet in this world of welterings
        And unease,
And that, while so, mechanic repetitions please ?

When shall I leave off doing these things ?—
        When I hear
You have dropped your dusty cloak and taken
        you wondrous wings
        To another sphere,
Where no pain is :  Then shall I hush this
        dinning gear.

# TO AN UNBORN PAUPER CHILD

## I

BREATHE not, hid Heart : cease silently,
And though thy birth-hour beckons thee,
    Sleep the long sleep :
    The Doomsters heap
Travails and teens around us here,
And Time-wraiths turn our songsingings to fear.

## II

Hark, how the peoples surge and sigh,
And laughters fail, and greetings die :
    Hopes dwindle ; yea,
    Faiths waste away,
Affections and enthusiasms numb ;
Thou canst not mend these things if thou dost
    come.

## III

Had I the ear of wombèd souls
Ere their terrestrial chart unrolls,
    And thou wert free
    To cease, or be,
Then would I tell thee all I know,
And put it to thee : Wilt thou take Life so ?

### IV

Vain vow !   No hint of mine may hence
To theeward fly :  to thy locked sense
    Explain none can
    Life's pending plan :
Thou wilt thy ignorant entry make
Though skies spout fire and blood and nations
        quake.

### V

Fain would I, dear, find some shut plot
Of earth's wide wold for thee, where not
    One tear, one qualm,
    Should break the calm.
But I am weak as thou and bare ;
No man can change the common lot to rare.

### VI

Must come and bide.   And such are we—
Unreasoning, sanguine, visionary—
    That I can hope
    Health, love, friends, scope
In full for thee ; can dream thou'lt find
Joys seldom yet attained by humankind !

# THE DEAD MAN WALKING

THEY hail me as one living,
    But don't they know
That I have died of late years,
    Untombed although ?

I am but a shape that stands here,
    A pulseless mould,
A pale past picture, screening
    Ashes gone cold.

Not at a minute's warning,
    Not in a loud hour,
For me ceased Time's enchantments
    In hall and bower.

There was no tragic transit,
    No catch of breath,
When silent seasons inched me
    On to this death. . . .

—A Troubadour-youth I rambled
    With Life for lyre,
The beats of being raging
    In me like fire.

136

But when I practised eyeing
    The goal of men,
It iced me, and I perished
    A little then.

When passed my friend, my kinsfolk
    Through the Last Door,
And left me standing bleakly,
    I died yet more ;

And when my Love's heart kindled
    In hate of me,
Wherefore I knew not, died I
    One more degree.

And if when I died fully
    I cannot say,
And changed into the corpse-thing
    I am to-day,

Yet is it that, though whiling
    The time somehow
In walking, talking, smiling,
    I live not now.

## " I LOOK INTO MY GLASS "

I LOOK into my glass,
And view my wasting skin,
And say, " Would God it came to pass
My heart had shrunk as thin ! "

For then, I, undistrest
By hearts grown cold to me,
Could lonely wait my endless rest
With equanimity.

But Time, to make me grieve,
Part steals, lets part abide ;
And shakes this fragile frame at eve
With throbbings of noontide

# EXEUNT OMNES

## I

EVERYBODY else, then, going,
And I still left where the fair was ? . . .
Much have I seen of neighbour loungers
　　Making a lusty showing,
　　Each now past all knowing.


## II

There is an air of blankness
In the street and the littered spaces ;
Thoroughfare, steeple, bridge and highway
　　Wizen themselves to lankness ;
　　Kennels dribble dankness.


## III

Folk all fade.　And whither,
As I wait alone where the fair was ?
Into the clammy and numbing night-fog
　　Whence they entered hither.
　　Soon one more goes thither.


*June* 2, 1913.

139

# AFTERWARDS

When the Present has latched its postern
  behind my tremulous stay,
    And the May month flaps its glad green
    leaves like wings,
Delicate-filmed as new-spun silk, will the neigh-
  bours say,
    " He was a man who used to notice such
    things " ?

If it be in the dusk when, like an eyelid's sound-
  less blink,
    The dewfall-hawk comes crossing the shades
    to alight
Upon the wind-warped upland thorn, a gazer
  may think,
    " To him this must have been a familiar
    sight."

If I pass during some nocturnal blackness,
  mothy and warm,
    When the hedgehog travels furtively over the
    lawn,
One may say, " He strove that such innocent
  creatures should come to no harm,
    But he could do little for them ; and now he
    is gone."

If, when hearing that I have been stilled at last,
    they stand at the door,
  Watching the full-starred heavens that winter
    sees,
Will this thought rise on those who will meet my
    face no more,
  " He was one who had an eye for such
    mysteries " ?

And will any say when my bell of quittance is
    heard in the gloom,
  And a crossing breeze cuts a pause in its
    outrollings,
Till they rise again, as they were a new bell's
    boom,
  " He hears it not now, but used to notice such
    things " ?

# PART II

## POEMS NARRATIVE AND
## REFLECTIVE

# PAYING CALLS

I WENT by footpath and by stile
   Beyond where bustle ends,
Strayed here a mile and there a mile,
   And called upon some friends.

On certain ones I had not seen
   For years past did I call,
And then on others who had been
   The oldest friends of all.

It was the time of midsummer
   When they had used to roam ;
But now, though tempting was the air,
   I found them all at home.

I spoke to one and other of them
   By mound and stone and tree
Of things we had done ere days were dim,
   But they spoke not to me.

# FRIENDS BEYOND

WILLIAM DEWY, Tranter Reuben, Farmer Led-
        low late at plough,
    Robert's kin, and John's, and Ned's,
And the Squire, and Lady Susan, lie in Mellstock
        churchyard now !

" Gone," I call them, gone for good, that group
        of local hearts and heads ;
    Yet at mothy curfew-tide,
And at midnight when the noon-heat breathes
        it back from walls and leads,

They've a way of whispering to me—fellow-
        wight who yet abide—
    In the muted, measured note
Of a ripple under archways, or a lone cave's
        stillicide :

" We have triumphed : this achievement turns
        the bane to antidote,
    Unsuccesses to success,
Many thought-worn eves and morrows to a
        morrow free of thought.

" No more need we corn and clothing, feel of old
        terrestrial stress ;
   Chill detraction stirs no sigh ;
Fear of death has even bygone us : death gave
        all that we possess."

*W. D.*—" Ye mid burn the old bass-viol that l
        set such value by."
*Squire*—" You may hold the manse in fee,
   You may wed my spouse, may let my
        children's memory of me die."

*Lady S.*—" You may have my rich brocades, my
        laces ; take each household key ;
   Ransack coffer, desk, bureau ;
   Quiz the few poor treasures hid there, con
        the letters kept by me."

*Far.*—" Ye mid zell my favourite heifer, ye mid
        let the charlock grow,
   Foul the grinterns, give up thrift."
*Far. Wife*—" If ye break my best blue china,
        children, I shan't care or ho."

*All*—" We've no wish to hear the tidings, how
        the people's fortunes shift ;
   What your daily doings are ;
   Who are wedded, born, divided ; if your
        lives beat slow or swift.

   " Curious not the least are we if our intents
        you make or mar,

If you quire to our old tune,
If the City stage still passes, if the weirs still
roar afar."

—Thus, with very gods' composure, freed those
crosses late and soon
Which, in life, the Trine allow
(Why, none witteth), and ignoring all that haps
beneath the moon,

William Dewy, Tranter Reuben, Farmer Led-
low late at plough,
Robert's kin, and John's, and Ned's,
And the Squire, and Lady Susan, murmur
mildly to me now.

# IN FRONT OF THE LANDSCAPE

PLUNGING and labouring on in a tide of visions,
  Dolorous and dear,
Forward I pushed my way as amid waste
      waters
      Stretching around,
Through whose eddies there glimmered the
      customed landscape
      Yonder and near

Blotted to feeble mist. And the coomb and
      the upland
      Coppice-crowned,
Ancient chalk-pit, milestone, rills in the grass-
      flat
      Stroked by the light,
Seemed but a ghost-like gauze, and no sub-
      stantial
      Meadow or mound.

What were the infinite spectacles featuring fore-
      most
      Under my sight,

Hindering me to discern my paced advancement,
    Lengthening to miles ;
What were the re-creations killing the daytime
    As by the night ?


O they were speechful faces, gazing insistent,
    Some as with smiles,
Some as with slow - born tears that brinily
        trundled
    Over the wrecked
Cheeks that were fair in their flush-time, ash
        now with anguish,
    Harrowed by wiles.


Yes, I could see them, feel them, hear them,
        address them—
    Halo-bedecked—
And, alas, onwards, shaken by fierce unreason,
    Rigid in hate,
Smitten by years-long wryness born of mis-
        prision,
    Dreaded, suspect.


Then there would breast me shining sights,
        sweet seasons
    Further in date ;
Instruments of strings with the tenderest
        passion
    Vibrant, beside
Lamps long extinguished, robes, cheeks, eyes
        with the earth's crust
    Now corporate.

Also there rose a headland of hoary aspect
        Gnawed by the tide,
Frilled by the nimb of the morning as two
        friends stood there
        Guilelessly glad—
Wherefore they knew not — touched by the
        fringe of an ecstasy
        Scantly descried.


Later images too did the day unfurl me,
        Shadowed and sad,
Clay cadavers of those who had shared in the
        dramas,
        Laid now at ease,
Passions all spent, chiefest the one of the broad
        brow
        Sepulture-clad.


So did beset me scenes, miscalled of the bygone,
        Over the leaze,
Past the clump, and down to where lay the
        beheld ones ;
        —Yea, as the rhyme
Sung by the sea - swell, so in their pleading
        dumbness
        Captured me these.


For, their lost revisiting manifestations
        In their live time
Much had I slighted, caring not for their purport,
        Seeing behind

Things more coveted, reckoned the better worth
      calling
        Sweet, sad, sublime.

Thus  do  they  now  show  hourly  before  the
      intenser
        Stare of the mind
As  they  were  ghosts  avenging  their  slights  by
      my bypast
        Body-borne eyes,
Show,  too,  with  fuller  translation  than  rested
      upon them
        As living kind.

Hence  wag  the  tongues  of  the  passing  people,
      saying
        In their surmise,
" Ah—whose  is  this  dull  form  that  perambu-
      lates, seeing nought
        Round him that looms
Whithersoever his footsteps turn in his farings,
        Save a few tombs ? "

# THE CONVERGENCE OF THE TWAIN

*(Lines on the loss of the " Titanic ")*

### I

In a solitude of the sea
Deep from human vanity,
And the Pride of Life that planned her, stilly
couches she.

### II

Steel chambers, late the pyres
Of her salamandrine fires,
Cold currents thrid, and turn to rhythmic tidal
lyres.

### III

Over the mirrors meant
To glass the opulent
The sea-worm crawls—grotesque, slimed, dumb,
indifferent.

### IV

Jewels in joy designed
To ravish the sensuous mind
Lie lightless, all their sparkles bleared and black
and blind.

153

V

Dim moon-eyed fishes near
Gaze at the gilded gear
And query : " What does this vaingloriousness
down here ? " . . .

VI

Well : while was fashioning
This creature of cleaving wing,
The Immanent Will that stirs and urges every-
thing

VII

Prepared a sinister mate
For her—so gaily great—
A Shape of Ice, for the time far and dissociate.

VIII

And as the smart ship grew
In stature, grace, and hue,
In shadowy silent distance grew the Iceberg too.

IX

Alien they seemed to be :
No mortal eye could see
The intimate welding of their later history,

### X

Or sign that they were bent
By paths coincident
On being anon twin halves of one august event,

### XI

Till the Spinner of the Years
Said " Now ! "  And each one hears,
And consummation comes, and jars two hemi-
spheres.

# THE SCHRECKHORN

(*With thoughts of Leslie Stephen*)

(June 1897)

ALOOF, as if a thing of mood and whim ;
Now that its spare and desolate figure gleams
Upon my nearing vision, less it seems
A looming Alp-height than a guise of him
Who scaled its horn with ventured life and limb,
Drawn on by vague imaginings, maybe,
Of semblance to his personality
In its quaint glooms, keen lights, and rugged
 trim.

At his last change, when Life's dull coils un-
 wind,
Will he, in old love, hitherward escape,
And the eternal essence of his mind
Enter this silent adamantine shape,
And his low voicing haunt its slipping snows
When dawn that calls the climber dyes them
 rose ?

# GEORGE MEREDITH

## (1828–1909)

Forty years back, when much had place
That since has perished out of mind,
I heard that voice and saw that face.

He spoke as one afoot will wind
A morning horn ere men awake ;
His note was trenchant, turning kind.

He was of those whose wit can shake
And riddle to the very core
The counterfeits that Time will break.

Of late, when we two met once more,
The luminous countenance and rare
Shone just as forty years before.

So that, when now all tongues declare
His shape unseen by his green hill,
I scarce believe he sits not there.

No matter.   Further and further still
Through the world's vaporous vitiate air
His words wing on—as live words will.

*May* 1909.

# A SINGER ASLEEP

*(Algernon Charles Swinburne, 1837–1909)*

### I

In this fair niche above the unslumbering sea,
That sentrys up and down all night, all day,
From cove to promontory, from ness to bay,
The Fates have fitly bidden that he should be
    Pillowed eternally.

### II

—It was as though a garland of red roses
Had fallen about the hood of some smug nun
When irresponsibly dropped as from the sun,
In fulth of numbers freaked with musical closes,
Upon Victoria's formal middle time
    His leaves of rhythm and rhyme.

### III

O that far morning of a summer day
When, down a terraced street whose pave-
    ments lay

Glassing the sunshine into my bent eyes,
I walked and read with a quick glad surprise
    New words, in classic guise,—


## IV

The passionate pages of his earlier years,
Fraught with hot sighs, sad laughters, kisses,
        tears ;
Fresh-fluted notes, yet from a minstrel who
Blew them not naïvely, but as one who knew
    Full well why thus he blew.


## V

I still can hear the brabble and the roar
At those thy tunes, O still one, now passed
        through
That fitful fire of tongues then entered new !
Their power is spent like spindrift on this shore ;
    Thine swells yet more and more.


## VI

—His singing-mistress verily was no other
Than she the Lesbian, she the music-mother
Of all the tribe that feel in melodies ;
Who leapt, love-anguished, from the Leucadian
        steep
Into the rambling world-encircling deep
    Which hides her where none sees.

### VII

And one can hold in thought that nightly here
His phantom may draw down to the water's
      brim,
And hers come up to meet it, as a dim
Lone shine upon the heaving hydrosphere,
And mariners wonder as they traverse near,
      Unknowing of her and him.

### VIII

One dreams him sighing to her spectral form :
" O teacher, where lies hid thy burning line ;
Where are those songs, O poetess divine
Whose very orts are love incarnadine ? "
And her smile back : " Disciple true and warm,
      Sufficient now are thine." . . .

### IX

So here, beneath the waking constellations,
Where the waves peal their everlasting strains,
And their dull subterrene reverberations
Shake him when storms make mountains of
      their plains—
Him once their peer in sad improvisations,
And deft as wind to cleave their frothy manes—
I leave him, while the daylight gleam declines
      Upon the capes and chines.

Bonchurch, 1910,

# IN THE MOONLIGHT

" O LONELY workman, standing there
In a dream, why do you stare and stare
At her grave, as no other grave there were ?

" If your great gaunt eyes so importune
Her soul by the shine of this corpse-cold moon,
Maybe you'll raise her phantom soon ! "

" Why, fool, it is what I would rather see
Than all the living folk there be ;
But alas, there is no such joy for me ! "

" Ah—she was one you loved, no doubt,
Through good and evil, through rain and
        drought,
And when she passed, all your sun went out ? "

" Nay : she was the woman I did not love,
Whom all the others were ranked above,
Whom during her life I thought nothing of."

# A CHURCH ROMANCE

(MELLSTOCK, *circa* 1835)

SHE turned in the high pew, until her sight
Swept the west gallery, and caught its row
Of music-men with viol, book, and bow
Against the sinking sad tower-window light.

She turned again ; and in her pride's despite
One strenuous viol's inspirer seemed to throw
A message from his string to her below,
Which said : " I claim thee as my own forth-
      right ! "

Thus their hearts' bond began, in due time
      signed.
And long years thence, when Age had scared
      Romance,
At some old attitude of his or glance
That gallery-scene would break upon her mind,
With him as minstrel, ardent, young, and trim,
Bowing " New Sabbath " or " Mount Ephraim."

# THE ROMAN ROAD

THE Roman Road runs straight and bare
As the pale parting-line in hair
Across the heath.   And thoughtful men
Contrast its days of Now and Then,
And delve, and measure, and compare ;

Visioning on the vacant air
Helmed legionaries, who proudly rear
The Eagle, as they pace again
                              The Roman Road.

But no tall brass-helmed legionnaire
Haunts it for me.   Uprises there
A mother's form upon my ken,
Guiding my infant steps, as when
We walked that ancient thoroughfare,
                              The Roman Road.

# THE OXEN

CHRISTMAS EVE, and twelve of the clock.
  " Now they are all on their knees,"
An elder said as we sat in a flock
  By the embers in hearthside ease.

We pictured the meek mild creatures where
  They dwelt in their strawy pen,
Nor did it occur to one of us there
  To doubt they were kneeling then.

So fair a fancy few would weave
  In these years !   Yet, I feel,
If some one said on Christmas Eve,
  " Come ; see the oxen kneel

" In the lonely barton by yonder coomb
  Our childhood used to know,"
I should go with him in the gloom,
  Hoping it might be so.

  1915.

# SHE HEARS THE STORM

THERE was a time in former years—
    While my roof-tree was his—
When I should have been distressed by fears
    At such a night as this !

I should have murmured anxiously,
    " The pricking rain strikes cold ;
His road is bare of hedge or tree,
    And he is getting old."

But now the fitful chimney-roar,
    The drone of Thorncombe trees,
The Froom in flood upon the moor,
    The mud of Mellstock Leaze,

The candle slanting sooty wick'd,
    The thuds upon the thatch,
The eaves-drops on the window flicked,
    The clacking garden-hatch,

And what they mean to wayfarers,
    I scarcely heed or mind ;
He has won that storm-tight roof of hers
    Which Earth grants all her kind.

# AFTER THE LAST BREATH

## (J. H. 1813–1904)

THERE'S no more to be done, or feared, or
    hoped ;
None now need watch, speak low, and list,
    and tire ;
No irksome crease outsmoothed, no pillow
    sloped
        Does she require.

Blankly we gaze.  We are free to go or stay ;
Our morrow's anxious plans have missed their
    aim ;
Whether we leave to-night or wait till day
        Counts as the same.

The lettered vessels of medicaments
Seem asking wherefore we have set them here ;
Each palliative its silly face presents
        As useless gear.

And yet we feel that something savours well ;
We note a numb relief withheld before ;

Our well-beloved is prisoner in the cell
      Of Time no more.

We see by littles now the deft achievement
Whereby she has escaped the Wrongers all,
In view of which our momentary bereavement
      Outshapes but small.

1904.

# NIGHT IN THE OLD HOME

When the wasting embers redden the chimney-
    breast,
And Life's bare pathway looms like a desert
    track to me,
And from hall and parlour the living have gone
    to their rest,
My perished people who housed them here come
    back to me.

They come and seat them around in their mouldy
    places,
Now and then bending towards me a glance of
    wistfulness,
A strange upbraiding smile upon all their faces,
And in the bearing of each a passive tristfulness.

" Do you uphold me, lingering and languishing
    here,
A pale late plant of your once strong stock ? "
    I say to them ;
" A thinker of crooked thoughts upon Life in
    the sere,
And on That which consigns men to night after
    showing the day to them ? "

" —O let be the Wherefore ! We fevered our
    years not thus :
Take of Life what it grants, without question ! "
    they answer me seemingly.
" Enjoy, suffer, wait : spread the table here
    freely like us,
And, satisfied, placid, unfretting, watch Time
    away beamingly ! "

# NEUTRAL TONES

WE stood by a pond that winter day,
And the sun was white, as though chidden of
 God,
And a few leaves lay on the starving sod ;
      —They had fallen from an ash, and were
      gray.

Your eyes on me were as eyes that rove
Over tedious riddles of years ago ;
And some words played between us to and fro
      On which lost the more by our love.

The smile on your mouth was the deadest thing
Alive enough to have strength to die ;
And a grin of bitterness swept thereby
      Like an ominous bird a-wing. . . .

Since then, keen lessons that love deceives,
And wrings with wrong, have shaped to me
Your face, and the God-curst sun, and a tree,
      And a pond edged with grayish leaves.

   1867.

# TO HIM

PERHAPS, long hence, when I have passed away,
Some other's feature, accent, thought like mine,
Will carry you back to what I used to say,
And bring some memory of your love's decline.

Then you may pause awhile and think, " Poor
     jade ! "
And yield a sigh to me—as ample due,
Not as the tittle of a debt unpaid
To one who could resign her all to you—

And thus reflecting, you will never see
That your thin thought, in two small words
     conveyed,
Was no such fleeting phantom-thought to me,
But the Whole Life wherein my part was played :
And you amid its fitful masquerade
A Thought—as I in your life seem to be !

  1866.

# ROME

(1887)

I SAT in the Muses' Hall at the mid of the day,
And it seemed to grow still, and the people to
pass away,
And the chiselled shapes to combine in a haze
of sun,
Till beside a Carrara column there gleamed forth
One.

She looked not this nor that of those beings
divine,
But each and the whole—an essence of all the
Nine ;
With tentative foot she neared to my halting-
place,
A pensive smile on her sweet, small, marvellous
face.

" Regarded so long, we render thee sad ? "
said she.
" Not you," sighed I, " but my own in-
constancy !

172

I worship each and each ; in the morning one,
And then, alas ! another at sink of sun.

" To-day my soul clasps Form ; but where is
my troth
Of yesternight with Tune : can one cleave to
both ? "
—" Be not perturbed," said she. " Though
apart in fame,
As I and my sisters are one, those, too, are the
same."

—" But my love goes further—to Story, and
Dance, and Hymn,
The lover of all in a sun-sweep is fool to whim—
Is swayed like a river-weed as the ripples run ! "
—" Nay, wooer, thou sway'st not. These are
but phases of one ;

" And that one is I ; and I am projected from
thee,
One that out of thy brain and heart thou causest
to be—
Extern to thee nothing. Grieve not, nor thy-
self becall,
Woo where thou wilt ; and rejoice thou canst
love at all ! "

# ROME

(1887)

Who, then, was Cestius,
And what is he to me ?—
Amid thick thoughts and memories multi-
tudinous
One thought alone brings he.

I can recall no word
Of anything he did ;
For me he is a man who died and was interred
To leave a pyramid

Whose purpose was exprest
Not with its first design,
Nor till, far down in Time, beside it found their
rest
Two countrymen of mine.

Cestius in life, maybe,
Slew, breathed out threatening ;
I know not.   This I know : in death all silently
He does a finer thing,

In beckoning pilgrim feet
With marble finger high
To where, by shadowy wall and history-haunted
street,
Those matchless singers lie. . . .

—Say, then, he lived and died
That stones which bear his name
Should mark, through Time, where two im-
mortal Shades abide ;
It is an ample fame.

# ON AN INVITATION TO THE UNITED STATES

## I

My ardours for emprize nigh lost
Since Life has bared its bones to me,
I shrink to seek a modern coast
Whose riper times have yet to be ;
Where the new regions claim them free
From that long drip of human tears
Which peoples old in tragedy
Have left upon the centuried years.

## II

For, wonning in these ancient lands,
Enchased and lettered as a tomb,
And scored with prints of perished hands,
And chronicled with dates of doom,
Though my own Being bear no bloom
I trace the lives such scenes enshrine,
Give past exemplars present room,
And their experience count as mine.

# AT A LUNAR ECLIPSE

Thy shadow, Earth, from Pole to Central Sea,
Now steals along upon the Moon's meek shine
In even monochrome and curving line
Of imperturbable serenity.

How shall I link such sun-cast symmetry
With the torn troubled form I know as thine,
That profile, placid as a brow divine,
With continents of moil and misery?

And can immense Mortality but throw
So small a shade, and Heaven's high human
     scheme
Be hemmed within the coasts yon arc implies?

Is such the stellar gauge of earthly show,
Nation at war with nation, brains that teem,
Heroes, and women fairer than the skies?

# THE SUBALTERNS

### I

" Poor wanderer," said the leaden sky,
   " I fain would lighten thee,
But there are laws in force on high
   Which say it must not be."


### II

—" I would not freeze thee, shorn one," cried
   The North, " knew I but how
To warm my breath, to slack my stride ;
   But I am ruled as thou."


### III

—" To-morrow I attack thee, wight,"
   Said Sickness. " Yet I swear
I bear thy little ark no spite,
   But am bid enter there."


### IV

—" Come hither, Son," I heard Death say ;
   " I did not will a grave

Should end thy pilgrimage to-day,
But I, too, am a slave ! "


v

We smiled upon each other then,
And life to me had less
Of that fell look it wore ere when
They owned their passiveness.

# THE SLEEP-WORKER

WHEN wilt thou wake, O Mother, wake and
    see—
As one who, held in trance, has laboured long
By vacant rote and prepossession strong—
The coils that thou hast wrought unwittingly ;

Wherein have place, unrealized by thee,
Fair growths, foul cankers, right enmeshed with
    wrong,
Strange orchestras of victim-shriek and song,
And curious blends of ache and ecstasy ?—

Should that morn come, and show thy opened
    eyes
All that Life's palpitating tissues feel,
How wilt thou bear thyself in thy surprise ?—

Wilt thou destroy, in one wild shock of shame,
Thy whole high heaving firmamental frame,
Or patiently adjust, amend, and heal ?

# BEYOND THE LAST LAMP

*(Near Tooting Common)*

### I

WHILE rain, with eve in partnership,
Descended darkly, drip, drip, drip,
Beyond the last lone lamp I passed
    Walking slowly, whispering sadly,
    Two linked loiterers, wan, downcast:
Some heavy thought constrained each face,
And blinded them to time and place.

### II

The pair seemed lovers, yet absorbed
In mental scenes no longer orbed
By love's young rays.   Each countenance
    As it slowly, as it sadly
    Caught the lamplight's yellow glance,
Held in suspense a misery
At things which had been or might be.

### III

When I retrod that watery way
Some hours beyond the droop of day,

Still I found pacing there the twain
    Just as slowly, just as sadly,
    Heedless of the night and rain.
One could but wonder who they were
And what wild woe detained them there.


IV

Though thirty years of blur and blot
Have slid since I beheld that spot,
And saw in curious converse there
    Moving slowly, moving sadly
    That mysterious tragic pair,
Its olden look may linger on—
All but the couple ; they have gone.


V

Whither ?   Who knows, indeed. . . . And yet
To me, when nights are weird and wet,
Without those comrades there at tryst
    Creeping slowly, creeping sadly,
    That lone lane does not exist.
There they seem brooding on their pain,
And will, while such a lane remain.

# THE DEAD QUIRE

### I

BESIDE the Mead of Memories,
Where Church-way mounts to Moaning Hill,
The sad man sighed his phantasies :
    He seems to sigh them still.

### II

" 'Twas the Birth-tide Eve, and the hamleteers
Made merry with ancient Mellstock zest,
But the Mellstock quire of former years
    Had entered into rest.

### III

" Old Dewy lay by the gaunt yew tree,
And Reuben and Michael a pace behind,
And Bowman with his family
    By the wall that the ivies bind.

### IV

" The singers had followed one by one,
Treble, and tenor, and thorough-bass ;
And the worm that wasteth had begun
    To mine their mouldering place.

### V

" For two-score years, ere Christ-day light,
Mellstock had throbbed to strains from these ;
But now there echoed on the night
    No Christmas harmonies.

### VI

" Three meadows off, at a dormered inn,
The youth had gathered in high carouse,
And, ranged on settles, some therein
    Had drunk them to a drowse.

### VII

" Loud, lively, reckless, some had grown,
Each dandling on his jigging knee
Eliza, Dolly, Nance, or Joan—
    Livers in levity.

### VIII

" The taper flames and hearthfire shine
Grew smoke-hazed to a lurid light,
And songs on subjects not divine
    Were warbled forth that night.

### IX

" Yet many were sons and grandsons here
Of those who, on such eves gone by,
At that still hour had throated clear
    Their anthems to the sky.

### x

" The clock belled midnight ; and ere long
One shouted, ' Now 'tis Christmas morn ;
Here's to our women old and young,
    And to John Barleycorn ! '

### XI

" They drink the toast and shout again :
The pewter-ware rings back the boom,
And for a breath-while follows then
    A silence in the room.

### XII

" When nigh without, as in old days,
The ancient quire of voice and string
Seemed singing words of prayer and praise
    As they had used to sing :

### XIII

" *While shepherds watch'd their flocks by night,*—
Thus swells the long familiar sound
In many a quaint symphonic flight
    To, *Glory shone around.*

### XIV

" The sons defined their fathers' tones,
The widow his whom she had wed,
And others in the minor moans
    The viols of the dead

### XV

" Something supernal has the sound
As verse by verse the strain proceeds,
And stilly staring on the ground
      Each roysterer holds and heeds.

### XVI

" Towards its chorded closing bar
Plaintively, thinly, waned the hymn,
Yet lingered, like the notes afar
      Of banded seraphim.

### XVII

" With brows abashed, and reverent tread,
The hearkeners sought the tavern door :
But nothing, save wan moonlight, spread
      The empty highway o'er.

### XVIII

" While on their hearing fixed and tense
The aerial music seemed to sink,
As it were gently moving thence
      Along the river brink.

### XIX

" Then did the Quick pursue the Dead
By crystal Froom that crinkles there ;
And still the viewless quire ahead
      Voiced the old holy air.

### XX

" By Bank-walk wicket, brightly bleached,
It passed, and 'twixt the hedges twain,
Dogged by the living ; till it reached
    The bottom of Church Lane.

### XXI

" There, at the turning, it was heard
Drawing to where the churchyard lay :
But when they followed thitherward
    It smalled, and died away.

### XXII

" Each headstone of the quire, each mound,
Confronted them beneath the moon ;
But no more floated therearound
    That ancient Birth-night tune.

### XXIII

" There Dewy lay by the gaunt yew tree,
There Reuben and Michael, a pace behind,
And Bowman with his family
    By the wall that the ivies bind. . . .

### XXIV

" As from a dream each sobered son
Awoke, and musing reached his door :
'Twas said that of them all, not one
    Sat in a tavern more."

### XXV

—The sad man ceased ; and ceased to heed
His listener, and crossed the leaze
From Moaning Hill towards the mead—
    The Mead of Memories.

1897.

# THE BURGHERS

## (17—)

THE sun had wheeled from Grey's to Dammer's
        Crest,
And still I mused on that Thing imminent :
At length I sought the High-street to the West.

The level flare raked pane and pediment
And my wrecked face, and shaped my nearing
        friend
Like one of those the Furnace held unshent.

" I've news concerning her," he said.   " Attend.
They fly to-night at the late moon's first gleam :
Watch with thy steel :  two righteous thrusts
        will end

Her shameless visions and his passioned dream.
I'll watch with thee, to testify thy wrong—
To aid, maybe.—Law consecrates the scheme."

I started, and we paced the flags along
Till I replied : " Since it has come to this
I'll do it !  But alone.  I can be strong."

Three hours past Curfew, when the Froom's
    mild hiss
Reigned sole, undulled by whirr of merchandize,
From Pummery-Tout to where the Gibbet is,

I crossed my pleasaunce hard by Glyd'path
    Rise,
And stood beneath the wall. Eleven strokes
    went,
And to the door they came, contrariwise,

And met in clasp so close I had but bent
My lifted blade on either to have let
Their two souls loose upon the firmament.

But something held my arm. " A moment yet
As pray-time ere you wantons die ! " I said ;
And then they saw me. Swift her gaze was set

With eye and cry of love illimited
Upon her Heart-king. Never upon me
Had she thrown look of love so thorough-
    sped ! . . .

At once she flung her faint form shieldingly
On his, against the vengeance of my vows ;
The which o'erruling. her shape shielded he.

Blanked by such love, I stood as in a drowse,
And the slow moon edged from the upland nigh,
My sad thoughts moving thuswise : " I may
    house

And I may husband her, yet what am I
But licensed tyrant to this bonded pair ?
Says Charity, Do as ye would be done by." . . .

Hurling my iron to the bushes there
I bade them stay.  And, as if brain and breast
Were passive, they walked with me to the stair.

Inside the house none watched ; and on we prest
Before a mirror, in whose gleam I read
Her beauty, his,—and mine own mien unblest ;

Till at her room I turned.  " Madam," I said,
" Have you the wherewithal for this ?  Pray
          speak.
Love fills no cupboard.  You'll need daily
          bread."

" We've nothing, sire," she lipped ;  " and
          nothing seek.
'Twere base in me to rob my lord unware ;
Our hands will earn a pittance week by week."

And next I saw she had piled her raiment rare
Within the garde-robes, and her household
          purse,
Her jewels, her least lace of personal wear,

And stood in homespun.  Now grown wholly
          hers,
I handed her the gold, her jewels all,
And him the choicest of her robes diverse.

" I'll take you to the doorway in the wall,
And then adieu," I told them.  " Friends,
    withdraw."
They did so ;  and she went—beyond recall.

And as I paused beneath the arch I saw
Their moonlit figures—slow, as in surprise—
Descend the slope, and vanish on the haw.

" ' Fool,' some will say," I thought —" But
    who is wise,
Save God alone, to weigh my reasons why ? "
—" Hast thou struck home ? " came with the
    boughs' night-sighs.

It was my friend.  " I have struck well.  They
    fly,
But carry wounds that none can cicatrize."
—" Not  mortal ? "  said  he.  " Lingering—
    worse," said I.

# THE CORONATION

At Westminster, hid from the light of day,
Many who once had shone as monarchs lay.

Edward the Pious, and two Edwards more,
The second Richard, Henrys three or four ;

That is to say, those who were called the
 Third,
Fifth, Seventh, and Eighth (the much self-
 widowered) ;

And James the Scot, and near him Charles the
 Second,
And, too, the second George could there be
 reckoned.

Of women, Mary and Queen Elizabeth,
And Anne, all silent in a musing death ;

And William's Mary, and Mary, Queen of Scots,
And consort - queens whose names oblivion
 blots ;

And several more whose chronicle one sees
Adorning ancient royal pedigrees.

—Now, as they drowsed on, freed from Life's
    old thrall,
And heedless, save of things exceptional,

Said one : " What means this throbbing
    thudding sound
That reaches to us here from overground ;

" A sound of chisels, augers, planes, and saws,
Infringing all ecclesiastic laws ?

" And these tons-weight of timber on us
    pressed,
Unfelt here since we entered into rest ?

" Surely, at least to us, being corpses royal,
A meet repose is owing by the loyal ? "

" —Perhaps a scaffold ! " Mary Stuart sighed,
" If such still be.  It was that way I died."

" —Ods !  Far more like," said he the many-
    wived,
" That for a wedding 'tis this work's contrived.

" Ha-ha !  I never would bow down to Rimmon,
But I had a rare time with those six women ! "

" Not all at once ? " gasped he who loved
    confession.
" Nay, nay ! " said Hal.  " That would have
    been transgression."

"—They build a catafalque here, black and tall,
Perhaps," mused Richard, " for some funeral ? "

And Anne chimed in :  " Ah, yes :  it may be
      so ! "
" Nay ! " squeaked Eliza.  " Little you seem
      to know—

" Clearly 'tis for some crowning here in state.
As they crowned us at our long bygone date ;

" Though we'd no such a power of carpentry,
But let the ancient architecture be ;

" If I were up there where the parsons sit,
In one of my gold robes, I'd see to it ! "

" But you are not," Charles chuckled.  " You
      are here,
And never will know the sun again, my dear ! "

" Yea," whispered those whom no one had
      addressed ;
" With slow, sad march, amid a folk distressed,
We were brought here, to take our dusty rest.

" And here, alas, in darkness laid below,
We'll wait and listen, and endure the show. . . .
Clamour dogs kingship ; afterwards not so ! "

1911.

# A COMMONPLACE DAY

THE day is turning ghost,
And scuttles from the kalendar in fits and
        furtively,
    To join the anonymous host
Of those that throng oblivion ; ceding his place,
        maybe,
    To one of like degree.


    I part the fire-gnawed logs,
Rake forth the embers, spoil the busy flames,
        and lay the ends
    Upon the shining dogs ;
Further and further from the nooks the twilight's
        stride extends,
    And beamless black impends.


    Nothing of tiniest worth
Have I wrought, pondered, planned ; no one
        thing asking blame or praise,
    Since the pale corpse-like birth
Of this diurnal unit, bearing blanks in all its
        rays—
    Dullest of dull-hued Days !

Wanly upon the panes
The rain slides, as have slid since morn my
    colourless thoughts ; and yet
Here, while Day's presence wanes,
And over him the sepulchre-lid is slowly lowered
    and set,
He wakens my regret.

Regret—though nothing dear
That I wot of, was toward in the wide world at
    his prime,
Or bloomed elsewhere than here,
To die with his decease, and leave a memory
    sweet, sublime,
Or mark him out in Time. . . .

—Yet, maybe, in some soul,
In some spot undiscerned on sea or land, some
    impulse rose,
Or some intent upstole
Of that enkindling ardency from whose maturer
    glows
The world's amendment flows ;

But which, benumbed at birth
By momentary chance or wile, has missed its
    hope to be
Embodied on the earth ;
And undervoicings of this loss to man's futurity
May wake regret in me.

# HER DEATH AND AFTER

THE summons was urgent : and forth I went—
By the way of the Western Wall, so drear
On that winter night, and sought a gate,
     Where one, by Fate,
   Lay dying that I held dear.

And there, as I paused by her tenement,
And the trees shed on me their rime and hoar,
I thought of the man who had left her lone—
     Him who made her his own
   When I loved her, long before.

The rooms within had the piteous shine
That home-things wear when there's aught
     amiss ;
From the stairway floated the rise and fall
     Of an infant's call,
   Whose birth had brought her to this.

Her life was the price she would pay for that
     whine—
For a child by the man she did not love.
" But let that rest for ever," I said,
     And bent my tread
   To the bedchamber above.

She took my hand in her thin white own,
And smiled her thanks—though nigh too weak—
And made them a sign to leave us there,
    Then faltered, ere
  She could bring herself to speak.


" Just to see you—before I go—he'll condone
Such a natural thing now my time's not
    much—
When Death is so near it hustles hence
    All passioned sense
  Between woman and man as such !


" My husband is absent.   As heretofore
The City detains him.   But, in truth,
He has not been kind. . . . I will speak no
    blame,
    But—the child is lame ;
  O, I pray she may reach his ruth !


" Forgive past days—I can say no more—
Maybe had we wed you would now repine ! . . .
But I treated you ill.   I was punished.   Farewell !
    —Truth shall I tell ?
  Would the child were yours and mine !


" As a wife I was true.   But, such my unease
That, could I insert a deed back in Time,
I'd make her yours, to secure your care ;
    And the scandal bear,
  And the penalty for the crime ! "

—When I had left, and the swinging trees
Rang above me, as lauding her candid say,
Another was I.   Her words were enough :
     Came smooth, came rough,
  I felt I could live my day.


Next night she died ;  and her obsequies
In the Field of Tombs where the earthworks
        frowned
Had her husband's heed.   His tendance spent,
     I often went
  And pondered by her mound.


All that year and the next year whiled,
And I still went thitherward in the gloam ;
But the Town forgot her and her nook,
     And her husband took
  Another Love to his home.


And the rumour flew that the lame lone child
Whom she wished for its safety child of mine,
Was treated ill when offspring came
     Of the new-made dame,
  And marked a more vigorous line.


A smarter grief within me wrought
Than even at loss of her so dear—
That the being whose soul my soul suffused
     Had a child ill-used,
  While I dared not interfere !

One eve as I stood at my spot of thought
In the white-stoned Garth, brooding thus her
             wrong,
Her husband neared ; and to shun his nod
         By her hallowed sod
     I went from the tombs among


To the Cirque of the Gladiators which faced—
That haggard mark of Imperial Rome,
Whose Pagan echoes mock the chime
         Of our Christian time
     From its hollows of chalk and loam.


The sun's gold touch was scarce displaced
From the vast Arena where men once bled,
When her husband followed ; bowed ; half-
             passed
         With lip upcast ;
     Then halting sullenly said :


" It is noised that you visit my first wife's tomb.
Now, I gave her an honoured name to bear
While living, when dead.   So I've claim to ask
         By what right you task
     My patience by vigiling there ?


" There's decency even in death, I assume ;
Preserve it, sir, and keep away ;
For the mother of my first-born you
         Show mind undue !
     —Sir, I've nothing more to say."

A desperate stroke discerned I then—
God pardon—or pardon not—the lie ;
She had sighed that she wished (lest the child
        should pine
        Of slights) 'twere mine,
    So I said : " But the father I.


" That you thought it yours is the way of men ;
But I won her troth long ere your day :
You learnt how, in dying, she summoned me ?
        'Twas in fealty.
    —Sir, I've nothing more to say,


" Save that, if you'll hand me my little maid,
I'll take her, and rear her, and spare you toil.
Think it more than a friendly act none can ;
        I'm a lonely man,
    While you've a large pot to boil.


" If not, and you'll put it to ball or blade—
To-night, to-morrow night, anywhen—
I'll meet you here. . . . But think of it,
        And in season fit
    Let me hear from you again."


—Well, I went away, hoping ;  but nought I
        heard
Of my stroke for the child, till there greeted me
A little voice that one day came
        To my window-frame
    And babbled innocently :

" My father who's not my own, sends word
I'm to stay here, sir, where I belong ! "
Next a writing came : " Since the child was the
            fruit
        Of your lawless suit,
    Pray take her, to right a wrong."

And I did.   And I gave the child my love,
And the child loved me, and estranged us none.
But compunctions loomed ; for I'd harmed the
            dead
        By what I said
    For the good of the living one.

—Yet though, God wot, I am sinner enough
And unworthy the woman who drew me so,
Perhaps this wrong for her darling's good
        She forgives, or would,
    If only she could know !

# A TRAMPWOMAN'S TRAGEDY

## (182–)

### I

From Wynyard's Gap the livelong day,
    The livelong day,
We beat afoot the northward way
    We had travelled times before.
The sun-blaze burning on our backs,
Our shoulders sticking to our packs,
By fosseway, fields, and turnpike tracks
    We skirted sad Sedge-Moor.

### II

Full twenty miles we jaunted on,
    We jaunted on,—
My fancy-man, and jeering John,
    And Mother Lee, and I.
And, as the sun drew down to west,
We climbed the toilsome Poldon crest,
And saw, of landskip sights the best,
    The inn that beamed thereby.

### III

For months we had padded side by side,
　　Ay, side by side
Through the Great Forest, Blackmoor wide,
　　And where the Parret ran.
We'd faced the gusts on Mendip ridge,
Had crossed the Yeo unhelped by bridge,
Been stung by every Marshwood midge,
　　I and my fancy-man.

### IV

Lone inns we loved, my man and I,
　　My man and I ;
" King's Stag," " Windwhistle " high and dry,
　　" The Horse " on Hintock Green,
The cosy house at Wynyard's Gap,
" The Hut " renowned on Bredy Knap,
And many another wayside tap
　　Where folk might sit unseen.

### V

Now as we trudged—O deadly day,
　　O deadly day !—
I teased my fancy-man in play
　　And wanton idleness.
I walked alongside jeering John,
I laid his hand my waist upon ;
I would not bend my glances on
　　My lover's dark distress

## VI

Thus Poldon top at last we won,
     At last we won,
And gained the inn at sink of sun
     Far-famed as " Marshal's Elm."
Beneath us figured tor and lea,
From Mendip to the western sea—
I doubt if finer sight there be
     Within this royal realm.

## VII

Inside the settle all a-row—
     All four a-row
We sat, I next to John, to show
     That he had wooed and won.
And then he took me on his knee,
And swore it was his turn to be
My favoured mate, and Mother Lee
     Passed to my former one.

## VIII

Then in a voice I had never heard,
     I had never heard,
My only Love to me : " One word,
     My lady, if you please !
Whose is the child you are like to bear ?—
*His* ?   After all my months o' care ? "
God knows 'twas not !   But, O despair !
     I nodded—still to tease.

### IX

Then up he sprung, and with his knife—
    And with his knife
He let out jeering Johnny's life,
    Yes ; there, at set of sun.
The slant ray through the window nigh
Gilded John's blood and glazing eye,
Ere scarcely Mother Lee and I
    Knew that the deed was done.

### X

The taverns tell the gloomy tale,
    The gloomy tale,
How that at Ivel-chester jail
    My Love, my sweetheart swung :
Though stained till now by no misdeed
Save one horse ta'en in time o' need ;
(Blue Jimmy stole right many a steed
    Ere his last fling he flung.)

### XI

Thereaft I walked the world alone,
    Alone, alone !
On his death-day I gave my groan
    And dropt his dead-born child.
'Twas nigh the jail, beneath a tree,
None tending me ; for Mother Lee
Had died at Glaston, leaving me
    Unfriended on the wild.

### XII

And in the night as I lay weak,
  As I lay weak,
The leaves a-falling on my cheek,
  The red moon low declined—
The ghost of him I'd die to kiss
Rose up and said : " Ah, tell me this !
Was the child mine, or was it his ?
  Speak, that I rest may find ! "


### XIII

O doubt not but I told him then,
  I told him then,
That I had kept me from all men
  Since we joined lips and swore.
Whereat he smiled, and thinned away
As the wind stirred to call up day . . .
—'Tis past !   And here alone I stray
  Haunting the Western Moor.


NOTES.—" Windwhistle " (Stanza IV.).   The highness
and dryness of Windwhistle Inn was impressed upon the
writer two or three years ago, when, after climbing on a
hot afternoon to the beautiful spot near which it stands
and entering the inn for tea, he was informed by the
landlady that none could be had, unless he would fetch
water from a valley half a mile off, the house containing
not a drop, owing to its situation.   However, a tantaliz-
ing row of full barrels behind her back testified to a
wetness of a certain sort, which was not at that time
desired.

" Marshal's Elm " (Stanza VI.), so   picturesquely

situated, is no longer an inn, though the house, or part of it, still remains. It used to exhibit a fine old swinging sign.

"Blue Jimmy" (Stanza x.) was a notorious horse-stealer of Wessex in those days, who appropriated more than a hundred horses before he was caught, among others one belonging to a neighbour of the writer's grandfather. He was hanged at the now demolished Ivel-chester or Ilchester jail above mentioned—that building formerly of so many sinister associations in the minds of the local peasantry, and the continual haunt of fever, which at last led to its condemnation. Its site is now an innocent-looking green meadow.

*April* 1902.

# THE DUEL

    " I ᴀᴍ here to time, you see ;
The glade is well - screened — eh ? — against
        alarm ;
    Fit place to vindicate by my arm
    The honour of my spotless wife,
    Who scorns your libel upon her life
      In boasting intimacy !

    " ' All hush-offerings you'll spurn,
My husband. Two must come ; one only go,'
    She said. ' That he'll be you I know ;
    To faith like ours Heaven will be just,
    And I shall abide in fullest trust
      Your speedy glad return.' "

    " Good. Here am also I ;
And we'll proceed without more waste of
        words
    To warm your cockpit. Of the swords
    Take you your choice. I shall thereby
    Feel that on me no blame can lie,
      Whatever Fate accords."

So stripped they there, and fought,
And the swords clicked and scraped, and the
        onsets sped ;
    Till the husband fell ; and his shirt was red
    With streams from his heart's hot cistern.
        Nought
    Could save him now ; and the other,
        wrought
    Maybe to pity, said :

    " Why did you urge on this ?
Your wife assured you ; and 't had better been
    That you had let things pass, serene
    In confidence of long-tried bliss,
    Holding there could be nought amiss
    In what my words might mean."

    Then, seeing nor ruth nor rage
Could move his foeman more—now Death's deaf
        thrall—
    He wiped his steel, and, with a call
    Like turtledove to dove, swift broke
    Into the copse, where under an oak
    His horse cropt, held by a page.

    " All's over, Sweet," he cried
To the wife, thus guised ; for the young page
        was she.
    " 'Tis as we hoped and said 't would be.
    He never guessed. . . . We mount and ride
    To where our love can reign uneyed.
    He's clay, and we are free."

# THE CARRIER

" THERE's a seat, I see, still empty ? "
    Cried the hailer from the road ;
" No, there is not ! " said the carrier,
    Quickening his horse and load.

" —They say you are in the grave, Jane ;
    But still you ride with me ! "
And he looked towards the vacant space
    He had kept beside his knee.

And the passengers murmured : " 'Tis where
    his wife
    In journeys to and fro
Used always to sit ; but nobody does
    Since those long years ago."

Rumble-mumble went the van
    Past Sidwell Church and wall,
Till Exon Towers were out of scan,
    And night lay over all.

# AN EAST-END CURATE

A SMALL blind street off East Commercial
    Road ;
    Window, door ; window, door ;
    Every house like the one before,
Is where the curate, Mr. Dowle, has found a
    pinched abode.
Spectacled, pale, moustache straw-coloured, and
    with a long thin face,
Day or dark his lodgings' narrow doorstep does
    he pace.

A bleached pianoforte, with its drawn silk
    plaitings faded,
Stands in his room, its keys much yellowed,
    cyphering, and abraded,
" Novello's Anthems " lie at hand, and also a
    few glees,
And " Laws of Heaven for Earth " in a frame
    upon the wall one sees.

He goes through his neighbours' houses as his
    own, and none regards,
And opens their back-doors off-hand, to look
    for them in their yards :

A man is threatening his wife on the other side
    of the wall,
But the curate lets it pass as knowing the
    history of it all.

Freely within his hearing the children skip and
    laugh and say :
    " There's    Mister    Dow - well !    There's
    Mister Dow-well ! " in their play ;
And the long, pallid, devoted face notes not,
But stoops along abstractedly, for good, or in
    vain, God wot !

## WAITING BOTH

A STAR looks down at me,
And says : " Here I and you
Stand, each in our degree :
What do you mean to do,—
     Mean to do ? "

I say : " For all I know,
Wait, and let Time go by,
Till my change come."—" Just so,"
The star says : " So mean I :—
     So mean I."

# THE SOMETHING THAT SAVED HIM

It was when
Whirls of thick waters laved me
Again and again,
That something arose and saved me ;
Yea, it was then.

In that day
Unseeing the azure went I
On my way,
And to white winter bent I,
Knowing no May.

Reft of renown,
Under the night clouds beating
Up and down,
In my needfulness greeting
Cit and clown.

Long there had been
Much of a murky colour
In the scene,
Dull prospects meeting duller ;
Nought between.

Last, there loomed
A closing-in blind alley,
Though there boomed
A feeble summons to rally
Where it gloomed.

The clock rang ;
The hour brought a hand to deliver ;
I upsprang,
And looked back at den, ditch and river,
And sang.

# " ACCORDING TO THE MIGHTY WORKING "

### I

WHEN moiling seems at cease
    In the vague void of night-time,
    And heaven's wide roomage stormless
    Between the dusk and light-time,
    And fear at last is formless,
We call the allurement Peace.

### II

Peace, this hid riot, Change,
    This revel of quick-cued mumming,
    This never truly being,
    This evermore becoming,
    This spinner's wheel onfleeing
Outside perception's range.

    1917.

# A NIGHT IN NOVEMBER

I MARKED when the weather changed,
And the panes began to quake,
And the winds rose up and ranged,
That night, lying half-awake.

Dead leaves blew into my room,
And alighted upon my bed,
And a tree declared to the gloom
Its sorrow that they were shed.

One leaf of them touched my hand,
And I thought that it was you
There stood as you used to stand,
And saying at last you knew !

(?) 1913.

# THE FALLOW DEER AT THE LONELY
# HOUSE

One without looks in to-night
  Through the curtain-chink
From the sheet of glistening white ;
One without looks in to-night
  As we sit and think
  By the fender-brink.

We do not discern those eyes
  Watching in the snow ;
Lit by lamps of rosy dyes
We do not discern those eyes
  Wondering, aglow,
  Fourfooted, tiptoe.

# THE SELFSAME SONG

A BIRD sings the selfsame song,
With never a fault in its flow,
That we listened to here those long
      Long years ago.

A pleasing marvel is how
A strain of such rapturous rote
Should have gone on thus till now
      Unchanged in a note !

—But it's not the selfsame bird.—
No : perished to dust is he. . . .
As also are those who heard
      That song with me.

# NEAR LANIVET, 1872

THERE was a stunted handpost just on the crest,
  Only a few feet high :
She was tired, and we stopped in the twilight-
    time for her rest,
  At the crossways close thereby.

She leant back, being so weary, against its stem,
  And laid her arms on its own,
Each open palm stretched out to each end of
    them,
  Her sad face sideways thrown.

Her white-clothed form at this dim-lit cease of
    day
  Made her look as one crucified
In my gaze at her from the midst of the dusty
    way,
  And hurriedly " Don't," I cried.

I do not think she heard.   Loosing thence she
    said,
  As she stepped forth ready to go,
" I am rested now.—Something strange came
    into my head ;
  I wish I had not leant so ! "

And wordless we moved onward down from the
    hill
    In the west cloud's murked obscure,
And looking back we could see the handpost
    still
    In the solitude of the moor.

" It struck her too," I thought, for as if afraid
    She heavily breathed as we trailed ;
Till she said, " I did not think how 'twould look
    in the shade,
    When I leant there like one nailed."

I, lightly : " There's nothing in it.   For *you*,
    anyhow ! "
    —" O I know there is not," said she . . .
" Yet I wonder . . . If no one is bodily
    crucified now,
    In spirit one may be ! "

And we dragged on and on, while we seemed to
    see
    In the running of Time's far glass
Her crucified, as she had wondered if she might
    be
    Some day.—Alas, alas !

# THE GARDEN SEAT

Its former green is blue and thin,
And its once firm legs sink in and in ;
Soon it will break down unaware,
Soon it will break down unaware.

At night when reddest flowers are black
Those who once sat thereon come back ;
Quite a row of them sitting there,
Quite a row of them sitting there.

With them the seat does not break down,
Nor winter freeze them, nor floods drown,
For they are as light as upper air,
They are as light as upper air !

# NIGHT-TIME IN MID-FALL

It is a storm-strid night, winds footing swift
    Through the blind profound ;
  I know the happenings from their sound ;
Leaves totter down still green, and spin and
    drift ;
The tree-trunks rock to their roots, which
    wrench and lift
The loam where they run onward underground.

The streams are muddy and swollen ; eels
    migrate
    To a new abode ;
  Even cross, 'tis said, the turnpike-road ;
(Men's feet have felt their crawl, home-coming
    late) :
The westward fronts of towers are saturate,
Church-timbers crack, and witches ride abroad.

# A SHEEP FAIR

THE day arrives of the autumn fair,
      And torrents fall,
Though sheep in throngs are gathered there,
      Ten thousand all,
Sodden, with hurdles round them reared :
And, lot by lot, the pens are cleared,
And the auctioneer wrings out his beard,
And wipes his book, bedrenched and
    smeared,
And rakes the rain from his face with the edge
    of his hand,
      As torrents fall.

The wool of the ewes is like a sponge
      With the daylong rain :
Jammed tight, to turn, or lie, or lunge,
      They strive in vain.
Their horns are soft as finger-nails,
Their shepherds reek against the rails,
The tied dogs soak with tucked-in tails,
The buyers' hat-brims fill like pails,
Which spill small cascades when they shift their
    stand
      In the daylong rain.

## Postscript

Time has trailed lengthily since met
    At Pummery Fair
Those panting thousands in their wet
    And woolly wear :
And every flock long since has bled,
And all the dripping buyers have sped,
And the hoarse auctioneer is dead,
Who " Going—going ! " so often said
As he consigned to doom each meek, mewed
    band
    At Pummery Fair.

# SNOW IN THE SUBURBS

EVERY branch big with it,
Bent every twig with it ;
Every fork like a white web-foot ;
Every street and pavement mute :
Some flakes have lost their way, and grope
back upward, when
Meeting those meandering down they turn and
descend again.
The palings are glued together like a wall,
And there is no waft of wind with the
fleecy fall.

A sparrow enters the tree,
Whereon immediately
A snow-lump thrice his own slight size
Descends on him and showers his head
and eyes.
And overturns him,
And near inurns him,
And lights on a nether twig, when its
brush
Starts off a volley of other lodging lumps with
a rush.

The steps are a blanched slope,
Up which, with feeble hope,
A black cat comes, wide-eyed and thin ;
And we take him in.

# FRAGMENT

At last I entered a long dark gallery,
  Catacomb-lined ; and ranged at the side
  Were the bodies of men from far and wide
Who, motion past, were nevertheless not dead.

  " The sense of waiting here strikes strong ;
Everyone's waiting, waiting, it seems to me ;
  What are you waiting for so long ?—
    What is to happen ? " I said.

" O we are waiting for one called God," said
      they,
  " (Though by some the Will, or Force, or
      Laws ;
  And, vaguely, by some, the Ultimate Cause ;)
Waiting for him to see us before we are clay.
  ·Yes ; waiting, waiting, for God *to know*
      *it*." . . .

  " To know what ? " questioned I.
" To know how things have been going on earth
      and below it :
  It is clear he must know some day."
  I thereon asked them why.

" Since he made us humble pioneers
Of himself in consciousness of Life's tears,
It needs no mighty prophecy
To tell that what he could mindlessly show
His creatures, he himself will know

" By some still close-cowled mystery
We have reached feeling faster than he,
But he will overtake us anon,
    If the world goes on."

# CYNIC'S EPITAPH

A RACE with the sun as he downed
    I ran at evetide,
Intent who should first gain the ground
    And there hide.

He beat me by some minutes then,
    But I triumphed anon,
For when he'd to rise up again
    I stayed on.

# IN DEATH DIVIDED

### I

I SHALL rot here, with those whom in their
 day
  You never knew,
And alien ones who, ere they chilled to clay,
  Met not my view,
Will in your distant grave-place ever neighbour
 you.

### II

No shade of pinnacle or tree or tower,
  While earth endures,
Will fall on my mound and within the hour
  Steal on to yours ;
One robin never haunt our two green covertures.


### III

Some organ may resound on Sunday noons
  By where you lie,
Some other thrill the panes with other tunes
  Where moulder I ;
No selfsame chords compose our common
 lullaby.

232

### IV

The simply-cut memorial at my head
  Perhaps may take
A rustic form, and that above your bed
  A stately make ;
No linking symbol show thereon for our tale's
  sake.

### V

And in the monotonous moils of strained,
  hard-run
  Humanity,
The eternal tie which binds us twain in one
  No eye will see
Stretching across the miles that sever you
  from me.

189–.

# IN TENEBRIS

" Considerabam ad dexteram, et videbam ; et non erat
qui cognosceret me. . . . Non est qui requirat animam
meam."—*Ps.* cxli.

WHEN the clouds' swoln bosoms echo back the
    shouts of the many and strong
That things are all as they best may be, save a
    few to be right ere long,
And my eyes have not the vision in them to
    discern what to these is so clear,
The blot seems straightway in me alone ;  one
    better he were not here.

The stout upstanders say, All's well with us :
    ruers have nought to rue !
And what the potent say so oft, can it fail to
    be somewhat true ?
Breezily go they, breezily come ;  their dust
    smokes around their career,
Till I think I am one born out of due time, who
    has no calling here.

Their dawns bring lusty joys, it seems ; their
evenings all that is sweet ;
Our times are blessed times, they cry : Life
shapes it as is most meet,
And nothing is much the matter ; there are
many smiles to a tear ;
Then what is the matter is I, I say. Why
should such an one be here ? . . .

Let him in whose ears the low-voiced Best is
killed by the clash of the First,
Who holds that if way to the Better there be, it
exacts a full look at the Worst,
Who feels that delight is a delicate growth
cramped by crookedness, custom, and fear,
Get him up and be gone as one shaped awry ;
he disturbs the order here.

1895-96

# "I HAVE LIVED WITH SHADES"

### I

I HAVE lived with Shades so long,
And talked to them so oft,
Since forth from cot and croft
I went mankind among,
  That sometimes they
  In their dim style
  Will pause awhile
  To hear my say ;

### II

And take me by the hand,
And lead me through their rooms
In the To-be, where Dooms
Half-wove and shapeless stand :
  And show from there
  The dwindled dust
  And rot and rust
  Of things that were.

### III

" Now turn," they said to me
One day : " Look whence we came,
And signify his name
Who gazes thence at thee."—

—" Nor name nor race
Know I, or can,"
I said, " Of man
So commonplace.

### IV

" He moves me not at all ;
I note no ray or jot
Of rareness in his lot,
Or star exceptional.
    Into the dim
    Dead throngs around
    He'll sink, nor sound
    Be left of him."

### V

" Yet," said they, " his frail speech,
Hath accents pitched like thine—
Thy mould and his define
A likeness each to each—
    But go !   Deep pain
    Alas, would be
    His name to thee,
    And told in vain ! "

*February* 2, 1899.

# A POET

ATTENTIVE eyes, fantastic heed,
Assessing minds, he does not need,
Nor urgent writs to sup or dine,
Nor pledges in the rosy wine.

For loud acclaim he does not care
By the august or rich or fair,
Nor for smart pilgrims from afar,
Curious on where his hauntings are.

But soon or later, when you hear
That he has doffed this wrinkled gear,
Some evening, at the first star-ray,
Come to his graveside, pause and say:

" Whatever his message—glad or grim—
Two bright-souled women clave to him ";
Stand and say that while day decays ;
It will be word enough of praise.

*July* 1914.

# PART III

## WAR POEMS, AND LYRICS FROM "THE DYNASTS"

# EMBARCATION

(*Southampton Docks : October* 1899)

HERE, where Vespasian's legions struck the
    sands,
And Cerdic with his Saxons entered in,
And Henry's army leapt afloat to win
Convincing triumphs over neighbour lands,

Vaster battalions press for further strands,
To argue in the selfsame bloody mode
Which this late age of thought, and pact, and
    code,
Still fails to mend.—Now deckward tramp the
    bands,

Yellow as autumn leaves, alive as spring ;
And as each host draws out upon the sea
Beyond which lies the tragical To-be,
None dubious of the cause, none murmuring,

Wives, sisters, parents, wave white hands and
    smile,
As if they knew not that they weep the while.

# DEPARTURE

*(Southampton Docks : October* 1899)

WHILE the far farewell music thins and fails,
And the broad bottoms rip the bearing brine—
All smalling slowly to the gray sea-line—
And each significant red smoke-shaft pales,

Keen sense of severance everywhere prevails,
Which shapes the late long tramp of mounting
    men
To seeming words that ask and ask again :
" How long, O striving Teutons, Slavs, and
    Gaels

Must your wroth reasonings trade on lives like
    these,
That are as puppets in a playing hand ?—
When shall the saner softer polities
Whereof we dream, have sway in each proud
    land
And patriotism, grown Godlike, scorn to stand
Bondslave to realms, but circle earth and seas ? "

# THE GOING OF THE BATTERY

## WIVES' LAMENT

*(November 2, 1899)*

### I

O IT was sad enough, weak enough, mad
  enough—
Light in their loving as soldiers can be—
First to risk choosing them, leave alone losing
  them
Now, in far battle, beyond the South Sea ! . . .

### II

Rain came down drenchingly ; but we un-
  blenchingly
Trudged on beside them through mirk and
  through mire,
They stepping steadily—only too readily !—
Scarce as if stepping brought parting-time
  nigher.

### III

Great guns were gleaming there, living things
  seeming there,
Cloaked in their tar-cloths, upmouthed to the
  night ;
Wheels wet and yellow from axle to felloe,
Throats blank of sound, but prophetic to sight.

IV

Gas-glimmers drearily, blearily, eerily
Lit our pale faces outstretched for one kiss,
While we stood prest to them, with a last quest
    to them
Not to court perils that honour could miss.


V

Sharp were those sighs of ours, blinded these
    eyes of ours,
When at last moved away under the arch
All we loved.   Aid for them each woman prayed
    for them,
Treading back slowly the track of their march.


VI

Someone said :  " Nevermore will they come :
    evermore
Are they now lost to us."   O it was wrong !
Though may be hard their ways, some Hand
    will guard their ways,
Bear them through safely, in brief time or long.


VII

—Yet, voices haunting us, daunting us, taunt-
    ing us,
Hint in the night-time when life beats are low
Other  and  graver  things. . . . Hold  we  to
    braver things,
Wait we  in trust, what Time's fulness shall show.

# DRUMMER HODGE

### I

THEY throw in Drummer Hodge, to rest
    Uncoffined—just as found :
His landmark is a kopje-crest
    That breaks the veldt around ;
And foreign constellations west
    Each night above his mound.

### II

Young Hodge the Drummer never knew—
    Fresh from his Wessex home—
The meaning of the broad Karoo,
    The Bush, the dusty loam,
And why uprose to nightly view
    Strange stars amid the gloam.

### III

Yet portion of that unknown plain
    Will Hodge for ever be ;
His homely Northern breast and brain
    Grow to some Southern tree,
And strange-eyed constellations reign
    His stars eternally.

# THE MAN HE KILLED

" Had he and I but met
  By some old ancient inn,
We should have sat us down to wet
  Right many a nipperkin !

" But ranged as infantry,
  And staring face to face,
I shot at him as he at me,
  And killed him in his place.

" I shot him dead because—
  Because he was my foe,
Just so : my foe of course he was ;
  That's clear enough ; although

" He thought he'd 'list, perhaps,
  Off-hand like—just as I—
Was out of work—had sold his traps—
  No other reason why.

" Yes ; quaint and curious war is !
  You shoot a fellow down
You'd treat if met where any bar is,
  Or help to half-a-crown."

1902.

# THE SOULS OF THE SLAIN

### I

THE thick lids of Night closed upon me
    Alone at the Bill
    Of the Isle by the Race [1]—
Many-caverned, bald, wrinkled of face—
And with darkness and silence the spirit was
      on me
    To brood and be still.

### II

No wind fanned the flats of the ocean,
    Or promontory sides,
    Or the ooze by the strand,
Or the bent-bearded slope of the land,
Whose base took its rest amid everlong motion
    Of criss-crossing tides.

### III

Soon from out of the Southward seemed
    nearing
    A whirr, as of wings
    Waved by mighty-vanned flies,
  Or by night-moths of measureless size,

[1] The " Race " is the turbulent sea-area off the Bill of
Portland, where contrary tides meet.

And in softness and smoothness well-nigh
     beyond hearing
          Of corporal things.


IV

     And they bore to the bluff, and alighted—
          A dim-discerned train
          Of sprites without mould,
     Frameless souls none might touch or might
          hold—
On the ledge by the turreted lantern, far-sighted
          By men of the main.


V

     And I heard them say " Home ! " and I
          knew them
          For souls of the felled
          On the earth's nether bord
     Under Capricorn, whither they'd warred,
And I neared in my awe, and gave heedfulness
          to them
          With breathings inheld.


VI

     Then, it seemed, there approached from the
          northward
          A senior soul-flame
          Of the like filmy hue :
     And he met them and spake : " Is it you,

O  my  men ? "  Said  they,  " Aye !   We  bear
homeward and hearthward
To feast on our fame ! "


### VII

" I've  flown  there  before  you,"  he  said
then :
" Your households are well ;
But—your kin linger less
On your glory and war-mightiness
Than  on  dearer  things."—" Dearer ? "  cried
these from the dead then,
" Of what do they tell ? "


### VIII

" Some mothers muse sadly, and murmur
Your doings as boys—
Recall the quaint ways
Of your babyhood's innocent days.
Some pray that, ere dying, your faith had grown
firmer,
And higher your joys.


### IX

A father broods :  ' Would I had set him
To some humble trade,
And so slacked his high fire,
And his passionate martial desire ;

And told him no stories to woo him and whet
        him
            To this dire crusade ! ' "


### X

" And, General, how hold out our sweet-
        hearts,
            Sworn loyal as doves ? "
            —" Many mourn ; many think
It is not unattractive to prink
Them in sables for heroes.  Some fickle and
        fleet hearts
            Have found them new loves."


### XI

" And    our    wives ? "   quoth    another
        resignedly,
            " Dwell they on our deeds ? "
            —" Deeds of home ; that live yet
Fresh as new—deeds of fondness or fret ;
Ancient words that were kindly expressed or
        unkindly,
            These, these have their heeds."


### XII

—" Alas !  then it seems that our glory
            Weighs less in their thought
            Than our old homely acts,
And the long-ago commonplace facts

Of our lives —held by us as scarce part of our
        story,
        And rated as nought ! "

### XIII

Then bitterly some : " Was it wise now
        To raise the tomb-door
        For such knowledge ?   Away ! "
But the rest : " Fame we prized till to-day ;
Yet that hearts keep us green for old kindness
        we prize now
        A thousand times more ! "

### XIV

Thus speaking, the trooped apparitions
        Began to disband
        And resolve them in two :
Those whose record was lovely and true
Bore to northward for home :  those of bitter
        traditions
        Again left the land,

### XV

And, towering to seaward in legions,
        They paused at a spot
        Overbending the Race—
That engulphing, ghast, sinister place—
Whither headlong they plunged, to the fathom-
        less regions
        Of myriads forgot.

### XVI

And the spirits of those who were homing
 Passed on, rushingly,
 Like the Pentecost Wind ;
And the whirr of their wayfaring thinned
And surceased on the sky, and but left in the
  gloaming
 Sea-mutterings and me.


*December* 1899.

# "MEN WHO MARCH AWAY"

(SONG OF THE SOLDIERS)

WHAT of the faith and fire within us
  Men who march away
  Ere the barn-cocks say
  Night is growing gray,
Leaving all that here can win us;
What of the faith and fire within us
  Men who march away?

Is it a purblind prank, O think you,
  Friend with the musing eye,
  Who watch us stepping by
  With doubt and dolorous sigh?
Can much pondering so hoodwink you!
Is it a purblind prank, O think you,
  Friend with the musing eye?

Nay. We well see what we are doing,
  Though some may not see—
  Dalliers as they be—
  England's need are we;
Her distress would leave us rueing:
Nay. We well see what we are doing,
  Though some may not see!

In our heart of hearts believing
    Victory crowns the just,
    And that braggarts must
    Surely bite the dust,
Press we to the field ungrieving,
In our heart of hearts believing
    Victory crowns the just.

Hence the faith and fire within us
    Men who march away
    Ere the barn-cocks say
    Night is growing gray,
Leaving all that here can win us;
Hence the faith and fire within us
    Men who march away.

*September* 5, 1914.

# BEFORE MARCHING AND AFTER

(In Memoriam F. W. G.)

Orion swung southward aslant
Where the starved Egdon pine-trees had
    thinned,
The Pleiads aloft seemed to pant
With the heather that twitched in the wind ;
But he looked on indifferent to sights such as
    these,
Unswayed by love, friendship, home joy or
    home sorrow,
And wondered to what he would march on the
    morrow.

The crazed household-clock with its whirr
Rang midnight within as he stood,
He heard the low sighing of her
Who had striven from his birth for his good ;
But he still only asked the spring starlight, the
    breeze,
What great thing or small thing his history
    would borrow
From that Game with Death he would play on
    the morrow.

When the heath wore the robe of late
   summer,
And the fuchsia-bells, hot in the sun,
Hung red by the door, a quick comer
Brought tidings that marching was done
For him who had joined in that game over-seas
Where Death stood to win, though his name
   was to borrow
A brightness therefrom not to fade on the
   morrow.

*September* 1915.

# JEZREEL

ON ITS SEIZURE BY THE ENGLISH UNDER
ALLENBY, SEPTEMBER 1918

DID they catch as it were in a Vision at shut
 of the day—
When their cavalry smote through the ancient
 Esdraelon Plain,
And they crossed where the Tishbite stood forth
 in his enemy's way—
His gaunt mournful Shade as he bade the King
 haste off amain ?

On war-men at this end of time—even on
 Englishmen's eyes—
Who slay with their arms of new might in that
 long-ago place,
Flashed he who drove furiously ? . . . Ah, did
 the phantom arise
Of that queen, of that proud Tyrian woman
 who painted her face ?

Faintly marked they the words " Throw her
 down ! " from the Night eerily,
Spectre-spots of the blood of her body on some
 rotten wall ?

And the thin note of pity that came : " A King's
    daughter is she,"
As they passed where she trodden was once by
    the chargers' footfall ?

Could such be the hauntings of men of to-day,
    at the cease
Of pursuit, at the dusk-hour, ere slumber their
    senses could seal ?
Enghosted seers, kings—one on horseback who
    asked " Is it peace ? " . . .
Yea, strange things and spectral may men have
    beheld in Jezreel !

*September* 24, 1918.

# IN TIME OF
## " THE BREAKING OF NATIONS "[1]

### I

ONLY a man harrowing clods
    In a slow silent walk
With an old horse that stumbles and nods
    Half asleep as they stalk.

### II

Only thin smoke without flame
    From the heaps of couch-grass ;
Yet this will go onward the same
    Though Dynasties pass.

### III

Yonder a maid and her wight
    Come whispering by ;
War's annals will cloud into night
    Ere their story die.

1915.                    [1] Jer. li. 20.

# FROM "THE DYNASTS"

## THE NIGHT OF TRAFALGÁR

*(Boatman's Song)*

### I

In the wild October night-time, when the wind
    raved round the land,
And the Back-sea met the Front-sea, and our
    doors were blocked with sand,
And we heard the drub of Dead-man's Bay,
    where bones of thousands are,
We knew not what the day had done for us at
    Trafalgár.
                Had done,
                Had done,
          For us at Trafalgár !

### II

" Pull hard, and make the Nothe, or down we
    go ! " one says, says he.
We pulled ;  and bedtime brought the storm ;
    but snug at home slept we.

Yet all the while our gallants after fighting
    through the day,
Were beating up and down the dark, sou'-west
    of Cadiz Bay.
            The dark,
            The dark,
        Sou'-west of Cadiz Bay !


## III

The victors and the vanquished then the storm
    it tossed and tore,
As hard they strove, those worn-out men, upon
    that surly shore ;
Dead Nelson and his half-dead crew, his foes
    from near and far,
Were rolled together on the deep that night at
    Trafalgár
            The deep,
            The deep,
        That night at Trafalgár !

# ALBUERA

THEY come, beset by riddling hail ;
They sway like sedges in a gale ;
They fail, and win, and win, and fail.   Albuera !

They gain the ground there, yard by yard,
Their brows and hair and lashes charred,
Their blackened teeth set firm and hard.

Their mad assailants rave and reel,
And face, as men who scorn to feel,
The close-lined, three-edged prongs of steel.

Till faintness follows closing-in,
When, faltering headlong down, they spin
Like leaves.  But those pay well who win
        Albuera.

Out of six thousand souls that sware
To hold the mount, or pass elsewhere,
But eighteen hundred muster there.

Pale Colonels, Captains, ranksmen lie,
Facing the earth or facing sky ;—
They strove to live, they stretch to die.

Friends, foemen, mingle ; heap and heap.—
Hide their hacked bones, Earth !—deep, deep,
    deep,
Where harmless worms caress and creep.

Hide their hacked bones, Earth !—deep, deep,
    deep,
Where harmless worms caress and creep.—
What man can grieve ? what woman weep ?
Better than waking is to sleep !   Albuera !

# HUSSAR'S SONG

### I

WHEN we lay where Budmouth Beach is,
  O, the girls were fresh as peaches,
With their tall and tossing figures and their eyes
    of blue and brown !
  And our hearts would ache with longing
  As we paced from our sing-songing,
With a smart *Clink ! Clink !* up the Esplanade
  and down.

### II

  They distracted and delayed us
  By the pleasant pranks they played us,
And what marvel, then, if troopers, even of
    regiments of renown,
  On whom flashed those eyes divine, O,
  Should forget the countersign, O,
As we tore *Clink ! Clink !* back to camp above
  the town.

264

## III

Do they miss us much, I wonder,
Now that war has swept us sunder,
And we roam from where the faces smile to
    where the faces frown ?
And no more behold the features
Of the fair fantastic creatures,
And no more *Clink! Clink!* past the parlours
    of the town ?

## IV

Shall we once again there meet them ?
Falter fond attempts to greet them ?
Will the gay sling-jacket glow again beside the
    muslin gown ?—
Will they archly quiz and con us
With a sideway glance upon us,
While our spurs *Clink! Clink!* up the Esplanade
    and down ?

# 'MY LOVE'S GONE A-FIGHTING'

*(Country-girl's Song)*

### I

My Love's gone a-fighting
  Where war-trumpets call,
The wrongs o' men righting
  Wi' carbine and ball,
And sabre for smiting,
  And charger, and all !

### II

Of whom does he think there
  Where war-trumpets call ?
To whom does he drink there,
  Wi' carbine and ball
On battle's red brink there,
  And charger, and all ?

### III

Her, whose voice he hears humming
  Where war-trumpets call,
" I wait, Love, thy coming
  Wi' carbine and ball,
And bandsmen a-drumming
  Thee, charger and all ! "

# THE EVE OF WATERLOO

*(Chorus of Phantoms)*

THE eyelids of eve fall together at last,
And the forms so foreign to field and tree
Lie down as though native, and slumber fast !

Sore are the thrills of misgiving we see
In the artless champaign at this harlequinade,
Distracting a vigil where calm should be !

The green seems opprest, and the Plain afraid
Of a Something to come, whereof these are the
      proofs,—
Neither earthquake, nor storm, nor eclipse's
      shade !

Yea, the coneys are scared by the thud of hoofs,
And their white scuts flash at their vanishing
      heels,
And swallows abandon the hamlet-roofs.

The mole's tunnelled chambers are crushed by
      wheels,
The lark's eggs scattered, their owners fled ;
And the hedgehog's household the sapper unseals.

The snail draws in at the terrible tread,
But in vain ; he is crushed by the felloe-rim ;
The worm asks what can be overhead,

And wriggles deep from a scene so grim,
And guesses him safe ; for he does not know
What a foul red flood will be soaking him !

Beaten about by the heel and toe
Are butterflies, sick of the day's long rheum,
To die of a worse than the weather-foe.

Trodden and bruised to a miry tomb
Are ears that have greened but will never be
      gold,
And flowers in the bud that will never bloom.

So the season's intent, ere its fruit unfold,
Is frustrate, and mangled, and made succumb,
Like a youth of promise struck stark and
      cold ! . . .

And what of these who to-night have come ?
—The young sleep sound ; but the weather
      awakes
In the veterans, pains from the past that numb ;

Old stabs of Ind, old Peninsular aches,
Old Friedland chills, haunt their moist mud bed;
Cramps from Austerlitz ; till their slumber
      breaks

And each soul sighs as he shifts his head
On the loam he's to lease with the other dead
From to-morrow's mist-fall till Time be sped !

# CHORUS OF THE PITIES

*(After the Battle)*

### SEMICHORUS I

To Thee whose eye all Nature owns,
Who hurlest Dynasts from their thrones,[1]
And liftest those of low estate
We sing, with Her men consecrate !

### II

Yea, Great and Good, Thee, Thee we hail,
Who shak'st the strong, Who shield'st the frail,
Who hadst not shaped such souls as we
If tendermercy lacked in Thee !

### I

Though times be when the mortal moan
Seems unascending to Thy throne,
Though seers do not as yet explain
Why Suffering sobs to Thee in vain ;

### II

We hold that Thy unscanted scope
Affords a food for final Hope,

[1] καθεῖλε ΔΥΝΑΣΤΑΣ ἀπὸ θρόνων.—*Magnificat.*

That mild-eyed Prescience ponders nigh
Life's loom, to lull it by-and-by.


I

Therefore we quire to highest height
The Wellwiller, the kindly Might
That balances the Vast for weal,
That purges as by wounds to heal.


II

The systemed suns the skies enscroll
Obey Thee in their rhythmic roll,
Ride radiantly at Thy command,
Are darkened by Thy Masterhand !


I

And these pale panting multitudes
Seen surging here, their moils, their moods,
All shall " fulfil their joy " in Thee,
In Thee abide eternally !


II

Exultant adoration give
The Alone, through Whom all living live,
The Alone, in Whom all dying die,
Whose means the End shall justify !   Amen.

# LAST CHORUS

## Semichorus I of the Years

Last as first the question rings
Of the Will's long travailings;
    Why the All-mover,
    Why the All-prover
Ever urges on and measures out the chordless
chime of Things.[1]


## II

    Heaving dumbly
    As we deem,
    Moulding numbly
    As in dream,
Apprehending not how fare the sentient subjects
of Its scheme.


## Semichorus I of the Pities

Nay ;—shall not Its blindness break ?
Yea, must not Its heart awake,

[1] Hor. *Epis.* i. 12.

271

Promptly tending
To Its mending
In a genial germing purpose, and **for loving-**
kindness' sake ?


## II

Should It never
Curb or cure
Aught whatever
Those endure
Whom It quickens, let them darkle to extinction
swift and sure.


### Chorus

But—a stirring thrills the air
Like to sounds of joyance there
That the rages
Of the ages
Shall be cancelled, and deliverance offered from
the darts that were,
Consciousness the Will informing, till It fashion
all things fair !

# APPENDIX I

## CRITICAL ADDITIONS

# A SIGN-SEEKER

I MARK the months in liveries dank and dry,
  The noontides many-shaped and hued ;
  I see the nightfall shades subtrude,
And hear the monotonous hours clang
    negligently by.

I view the evening bonfires of the sun
  On hills where morning rains have hissed ;
  The eyeless countenance of the mist
Pallidly rising when the summer droughts are
    done.

I have seen the lightning-blade, the leaping star,
  The cauldrons of the sea in storm,
  Have felt the earthquake's lifting arm,
And trodden where abysmal fires and snow-
    cones are.

I learn to prophesy the hid eclipse,
  The coming of eccentric orbs ;
  To mete the dust the sky absorbs,
To weigh the sun, and fix the hour each planet
    dips.

I witness fellow earth-men surge and strive ;
  Assemblies meet, and throb, and part ;
  Death's sudden finger, sorrow's smart ;
—All the vast various moils that mean a world
  alive.

But that I fain would wot of shuns my sense—
  Those sights of which old prophets tell,
  Those signs the general word so well
As vouchsafed their unheed, denied my long
  suspense.

In graveyard green, where his pale dust lies pent
  To glimpse a phantom parent, friend,
  Wearing his smile, and " Not the end ! "
Outbreathing softly : that were blest
  enlightenment ;

Or, if a dead Love's lips, whom dreams reveal
  When midnight imps of King Decay
  Delve sly to solve me back to clay,
Should leave some print to prove her spirit-
  kisses real ;

Or, when Earth's Frail lie bleeding of her
  Strong,
  If some Recorder, as in Writ,
  Near to the weary scene should flit
And drop one plume as pledge that Heaven
  inscrolls the wrong.

—There are who, rapt to heights of trancelike
  trust,

These tokens claim to feel and see,
  Read radiant hints of times to be—
Of heart to heart returning after dust to dust.

Such scope is granted not to lives like mine . . .
  I have lain in dead men's beds, have walked
  The tombs of those with whom I had talked,
Called many a gone and goodly one to shape a
    sign,

And panted for response. But none replies ;
  No warnings loom, nor whisperings
  To open out my limitings,
And Nescience mutely muses : When a man falls
    he lies.

# NATURE'S QUESTIONING

When I look forth at dawning, pool,
    Field, flock, and lonely tree,
    All seem to gaze at me
Like chastened children sitting silent in a
    school ;

Their faces dulled, constrained, and worn,
    As though the master's ways
    Through the long teaching days
Had cowed them till their early zest was over-
    borne.

Upon them stirs in lippings mere
    (As if once clear in call,
    But now scarce breathed at all)—
" We wonder, ever wonder, why we find us
    here !

" Has some Vast Imbecility,
    Mighty to build and blend,
    But impotent to tend,
Framed us in jest, and left us now to hazardry ?

" Or come we of an Automaton
    Unconscious of our pains ? . . .
    Or are we live remains
Of Godhead dying downwards, brain and eye
    now gone ?

" Or is it that some high Plan betides,
　　　As yet not understood,
　　　Of Evil stormed by Good,
We the Forlorn Hope over which Achievement
　　　strides ? "

Thus things around. No answerer I. . . .
　　　Meanwhile the winds, and rains,
　　　And Earth's old glooms and pains
Are still the same, and Life and Death are
　　　neighbours nigh.

# THE IMPERCIPIENT

*(At a Cathedral Service)*

THAT with this bright believing band
    I have no claim to be,
That faiths by which my comrades stand
    Seem fantasies to me,
And mirage-mists their Shining Land,
    Is a strange destiny.

Why thus my soul should be consigned
    To infelicity,
Why always I must feel as blind
    To sights my brethren see,
Why joys they've found I cannot find,
    Abides a mystery.

Since heart of mine knows not that ease
    Which they know ; since it be
That He who breathes All's Well to these
    Breathes no All's-Well to me,
My lack might move their sympathies
    And Christian charity !

I am like a gazer who should mark
    An inland company
Standing upfingered, with, " Hark ! hark !
    The glorious distant sea ! "
And feel, " Alas, 'tis but yon dark
    And wind-swept pine to me ! "

Yet I would bear my shortcomings
    With meet tranquillity,
But for the charge that blessed things
    I'd liefer not have be.
O, doth a bird deprived of wings
    Go earth-bound wilfully !

         .      .      .

Enough. As yet disquiet clings
    About us. Rest shall we.

# AN AUGUST MIDNIGHT

### I

A SHADED lamp and a waving blind,
And the beat of a clock from a distant floor :
On this scene enter—winged, horned, and
   spined—
A longlegs, a moth, and a dumbledore ;
While 'mid my page there idly stands
A sleepy fly, that rubs its hands. . . .

### II

Thus meet we five, in this still place,
At this point of time, at this point in space.
—My guests besmear my new-penned line,
Or bang at the lamp and fall supine.
" God's humblest, they ! " I muse. Yet why ?
They know Earth-secrets that know not I.

   *Max Gate, 1899*

# THE RUINED MAID

" O 'MELIA, my dear, this does everything
  crown !
Who could have supposed I should meet you in
  Town ?
And whence such fair garments, such
  prosperi-ty ? "—
" O didn't you know I'd been ruined ? " said she.

—" You left us in tatters, without shoes or socks,
Tired of digging potatoes, and spudding up
  docks ;
And now you've gay bracelets and bright
  feathers three ! "—
" Yes : that's how we dress when we're ruined,"
  said she.

—" At home in the barton you said ' thee ' and
  ' thou ',
And ' thik oon ', and ' theäs oon ', and ' t'other ';
  but now
Your talking quite fits 'ee for high
  compa-ny ! "—
" Some polish is gained with one's ruin," said
  she.

—" Your hands were like paws then, your face
  blue and bleak
But now I'm bewitched by your delicate cheek,
And your little gloves fit as on any la-dy ! "—
" We never do work when we're ruined," said she.

—" You used to call home-life a hag-ridden
  dream,
And you'd sigh, and you'd sock ; but at present
  you seem
To know not of megrims or melancho-ly ! "—
" True. One's pretty lively when ruined," said
  she.

—" I wish I had feathers, a fine sweeping gown,
And a delicate face, and could strut about
  Town ! "—
" My dear—a raw country girl, such as you be,
Cannot quite expect that. You ain't ruined," said
  she.

*Westbourne Park Villas, 1866*

# CHANNEL FIRING

THAT night your great guns, unawares,
Shook all our coffins as we lay,
And broke the chancel window-squares,
We thought it was the Judgment-day

And sat upright. While drearisome
Arose the howl of wakened hounds:
The mouse let fall the altar-crumb,
The worms drew back into the mounds,

The glebe cow drooled. Till God called, " No ;
It's gunnery practice out at sea
Just as before you went below ;
The world is as it used to be :

" All nations striving strong to make
Red war yet redder. Mad as hatters
They do no more for Christés sake
Than you who are helpless in such matters.

" That this is not the judgment-hour
For some of them's a blessed thing,
For if it were they'd have to scour
Hell's floor for so much threatening. . . .

" Ha, ha. It will be warmer when
I blow the trumpet (if indeed
I ever do ; for you are men,
And rest eternal sorely need)."

So down we lay again. " I wonder,
Will the world ever saner be,"
Said one, " than when He sent us under
In our indifferent century ! "

And many a skeleton shook his head.
" Instead of preaching forty year,"
My neighbour Parson Thirdly said,
" I wish I had stuck to pipes and beer."

Again the guns disturbed the hour,
Roaring their readiness to avenge,
As far inland as Stourton Tower,
And Camelot, and starlit Stonehenge.

*April 1914*

# A PLAINT TO MAN

When you slowly emerged from the den of Time,
And gained percipience as you grew,
And fleshed you fair out of shapeless slime,

Wherefore, O Man, did there come to you
The unhappy need of creating me—
A form like your own—for praying to ?

My virtue, power, utility,
Within my maker must all abide,
Since none in myself can ever be,

One thin as a phasm on a lantern-slide
Shown forth in the dark upon some dim sheet,
And by none but its showman vivified.

" Such a forced device," you may say, " is meet
For easing a loaded heart at whiles :
Man needs to conceive of a mercy-seat

Somewhere above the gloomy aisles
Of this wailful world, or he could not bear
The irk no local hope beguiles."

—But since I was framed in your first despair
The doing without me has had no play
In the minds of men when shadows scare ;

And now that I dwindle day by day
Beneath the deicide eyes of seers
In a light that will not let me stay,

And to-morrow the whole of me disappears,
The truth should be told, and the fact be faced
That had best been faced in earlier years :

The fact of life with dependence placed
On the human heart's resource alone,
In brotherhood bonded close and graced

With loving-kindness fully blown,
And visioned help unsought, unknown.

*1909–10*

# UNDER THE WATERFALL

" WHENEVER I plunge my arm, like this,
In a basin of water, I never miss
The sweet sharp sense of a fugitive day
Fetched back from its thickening shroud of gray.
      Hence the only prime
      And real love-rhyme
      That I know by heart,
      And that leaves no smart,
Is the purl of a little valley fall
About three spans wide and two spans tall
Over a table of solid rock,
And into a scoop of the self-same block ;
The purl of a runlet that never ceases
In stir of kingdoms, in wars, in peaces ;
With a hollow boiling voice it speaks
And has spoken since hills were turfless peaks."

" And why gives this the only prime
Idea to you of a real love-rhyme ?
And why does plunging your arm in a bowl
Full of spring water, bring throbs to your soul ? "

" Well, under the fall, in a crease of the stone,
Though where precisely none ever has known,
Jammed darkly, nothing to show how prized,
And by now with its smoothness opalized,
       Is a drinking-glass :
       For, down that pass
       My lover and I
       Walked under a sky
Of blue with a leaf-wove awning of green,
In the burn of August, to paint the scene,
And we placed our basket of fruit and wine
By the runlet's rim, where we sat to dine ;
And when we had drunk from the glass together,
Arched by the oak-copse from the weather,
I held the vessel to rinse in the fall,
Where it slipped, and sank, and was past recall,
Though we stooped and plumbed the little abyss
With long bared arms. There the glass still is.
And, as said, if I thrust my arm below
Cold water in basin or bowl, a throe
From the past awakens a sense of that time,
And the glass we used, and the cascade's rhyme.
The basin seems the pool, and its edge
The hard smooth face of the brook-side ledge,
And the leafy pattern of china-ware
The hanging plants that were bathing there.

" By night, by day, when it shines or lours,
There lies intact that chalice of ours,
And its presence adds to the rhyme of love
Persistently sung by the fall above.
No lip has touched it since his and mine
In turns therefrom sipped lovers' wine."

# TRANSFORMATIONS

PORTION of this yew
Is a man my grandsire knew,
Bosomed here at its foot :
This branch may be his wife,
A ruddy human life
Now turned to a green shoot.

These grasses must be made
Of her who often prayed,
Last century, for repose ;
And the fair girl long ago
Whom I often tried to know
May be entering this rose.

So, they are not underground,
But as nerves and veins abound
In the growths of upper air,
And they feel the sun and rain,
And the energy again
That made them what they were !

# OVERLOOKING THE RIVER STOUR

THE swallows flew in the curves of an eight
        Above the river-gleam
        In the wet June's last beam :
Like little crossbows animate
The swallows flew in the curves of an eight
        Above the river-gleam.

Planing up shavings of crystal spray
        A moor-hen darted out
        From the bank thereabout,
And through the stream-shine ripped his way ;
Planing up shavings of crystal spray
        A moor-hen darted out.

Closed were the kingcups ; and the mead
        Dripped in monotonous green,
        Though the day's morning sheen
Had shown it golden and honeybee'd ;
Closed were the kingcups ; and the mead
        Dripped in monotonous green.

And never I turned my head, alack,
        While these things met my gaze
        Through the pane's drop-drenched
        glaze,
To see the more behind my back. . . .
O never I turned, but let, alack,
        These less things hold my gaze !

# OLD FURNITURE

I KNOW not how it may be with others
 Who sit amid relics of householdry
That date from the days of their mothers'
   mothers,
 But well I know how it is with me
  Continually.

I see the hands of the generations
 That owned each shiny familiar thing
In play on its knobs and indentations,
 And with its ancient fashioning
  Still dallying :

Hands behind hands, growing paler and paler,
 As in a mirror a candle-flame
Shows images of itself, each frailer
 As it recedes, though the eye may frame
  Its shape the same.

On the clock's dull dial a foggy finger,
 Moving to set the minutes right
With tentative touches that lift and linger
 In the wont of a moth on a summer night,
  Creeps to my sight.

On this old viol, too, fingers are dancing—
    As whilom—just over the strings by the nut,
The tip of a bow receding, advancing
    In airy quivers, as if it would cut
      The plaintive gut.

And I see a face by that box for tinder,
    Glowing forth in fits from the dark,
And fading again, as the linten cinder
    Kindles to red at the flinty spark,
      Or goes out stark.

Well, well. It is best to be up and doing,
    The world has no use for one to-day
Who eyes things thus—no aim pursuing !
    He should not continue in this stay,
      But sink away.

# DURING WIND AND RAIN

THEY sing their dearest songs—
He, she, all of them—yea,
Treble and tenor and bass,
   And one to play ;
With the candles mooning each face. . . .
   Ah, no ; the years O !
How the sick leaves reel down in throngs !

They clear the creeping moss—
Elders and juniors—aye,
Making the pathways neat
   And the garden gay ;
And they build a shady seat. . . .
   Ah, no ; the years, the years ;
See, the white storm-birds wing across !

They are blithely breakfasting all—
Men and maidens—yea,
Under the summer tree,
   With a glimpse of the bay,
While pet fowl come to the knee. . . .
   Ah, no ; the years O !
And the rotten rose is ript from the wall.

They change to a high new house,
He, she, all of them—aye,
Clocks and carpets and chairs
    On the lawn all day,
And brightest things that are theirs. . . .
    Ah, no ; the years, the years ;
Down their carved names the rain-drop ploughs.

# THE SHADOW ON THE STONE

I went by the Druid stone
That broods in the garden white and lone,
And I stopped and looked at the shifting shadows
   That at some moments fall thereon
   From the tree hard by with a rhythmic swing,
   And they shaped in my imagining
To the shade that a well-known head and
       shoulders
   Threw there when she was gardening.

I thought her behind my back,
   Yea, her I long had learned to lack,
And I said : " I am sure you are standing behind
       me,
   Though how do you get into this old track ? "
   And there was no sound but the fall of a leaf
   As a sad response; and to keep down grief
I would not turn my head to discover
   That there was nothing in my belief.

Yet I wanted to look and see
   That nobody stood at the back of me ;
But I thought once more : " Nay, I'll not
       unvision

297

A shape which, somehow, there may be. ''
So I went on softly from the glade,
And left her behind me throwing her shade,
As she were indeed an apparition—
My head unturned lest my dream should fade.

*Begun 1913: finished 1916*

# HE RESOLVES TO SAY NO MORE

O MY soul, keep the rest unknown !
It is too like a sound of moan
      When the charnel-eyed
      Pale Horse has nighed :
Yea, none shall gather what I hide !

Why load men's minds with more to bear
That bear already ails to spare ?
      From now alway
      Till my last day
What I discern I will not say.

Let Time roll backward if it will ;
(Magians who drive the midnight quill
      With brain aglow
      Can see it so,)
What I have learnt no man shall know.

And if my vision range beyond
The blinkered sight of souls in bond,
      —By truth made free—
      I'll let all be,
And show to no man what I see.

# APPENDIX II

## POEMS OF 1912–13

*Veteris vestigia flammae*

# THE GOING

WHY did you give no hint that night
That quickly after the morrow's dawn,
And calmly, as if indifferent quite,
You would close your term here, up and be gone
      Where I could not follow
      With wing of swallow
To gain one glimpse of you ever anon !

      Never to bid good-bye,
      Or lip me the softest call,
Or utter a wish for a word, while I
Saw morning harden upon the wall,
      Unmoved, unknowing
      That your great going
Had place that moment, and altered all.

Why do you make me leave the house
And think for a breath it is you I see
At the end of the alley of bending boughs
Where so often at dusk you used to be ;
      Till in darkening dankness
      The yawning blankness
Of the perspective sickens me !

                You were she who abode
                By those red-veined rocks far West,
You were the swan-necked one who rode
Along the beetling Beeny Crest,
                And, reining nigh me,
                Would muse and eye me,
While Life unrolled us its very best.

Why, then, latterly did we not speak,
Did we not think of those days long dead,
And ere your vanishing strive to seek
That time's renewal ? We might have said,
                " In this bright spring weather
                We'll visit together
Those places that once we visited."

                Well, well ! All's past amend,
                Unchangeable. It must go.
I seem but a dead man held on end
To sink down soon. . . . O you could not know
                That such swift fleeing
                No soul foreseeing—
Not even I—would undo me so !

   *December 1912*

# YOUR LAST DRIVE

HERE by the moorway you returned,
And saw the borough lights ahead
That lit your face—all undiscerned
To be in a week the face of the dead,
And you told of the charm of that haloed view
That never again would beam on you.

And on your left you passed the spot
Where eight days later you were to lie,
And be spoken of as one who was not ;
Beholding it with a heedless eye
As alien from you, though under its tree
You soon would halt everlastingly.

I drove not with you. . . . Yet had I sat
At your side that eve I should not have seen
That the countenance I was glancing at
Had a last-time look in the flickering sheen,
Nor have read the writing upon your face,
" I go hence soon to my resting-place ;

" You may miss me then. But I shall not know
How many times you visit me there,
Or what your thoughts are, or if you go
There never at all. And I shall not care.
Should you censure me I shall take no heed,
And even your praises no more shall need. "

True : never you'll know. And you will not mind.
But shall I then slight you because of such ?
Dear ghost, in the past did you ever find
The thought " What profit, " move me much ?
Yet abides the fact, indeed, the same,—
You are past love, praise, indifference, blame.

*December 1912*

# THE WALK

You did not walk with me
Of late to the hill-top tree
    By the gated ways,
    As in earlier days ;
    You were weak and lame,
    So you never came,
And I went alone, and I did not mind,
Not thinking of you as left behind.

I walked up there to-day
Just in the former way ;
    Surveyed around
    The familiar ground
    By myself again :
    What difference, then ?
Only that underlying sense
Of the look of a room on returning thence.

# RAIN ON A GRAVE

Clouds spout upon her
   Their waters amain
   In ruthless disdain,—
Her who but lately
   Had shivered with pain
As at touch of dishonour
If there had lit on her
So coldly, so straightly
   Such arrows of rain :

One who to shelter
   Her delicate head
Would quicken and quicken
   Each tentative tread
If drops chanced to pelt her
   That summertime spills
   In dust-paven rills
When thunder-clouds thicken
   And birds close their bills.

Would that I lay there
   And she were housed here !
Or better, together
Were folded away there
Exposed to one weather

We both,—who would stray there
When sunny the day there,
 Or evening was clear
 At the prime of the year.

Soon will be growing
 Green blades from her mound,
And daisies be showing
 Like stars on the ground,
Till she form part of them—
Ay—the sweet heart of them,
Loved beyond measure
With a child's pleasure
 All her life's round.

*31 Jan. 1913*

## " I FOUND HER OUT THERE "

I FOUND her out there
On a slope few see,
That falls westwardly
To the salt-edged air,
Where the ocean breaks
On the purple strand,
And the hurricane shakes
The solid land.

I brought her here,
And have laid her to rest
In a noiseless nest
No sea beats near.
She will never be stirred
In her loamy cell
By the waves long heard
And loved so well.

So she does not sleep
By those haunted heights
The Atlantic smites
And the blind gales sweep,
Whence she often would gaze
At Dundagel's fanned head,
While the dipping blaze
Dyed her face fire-red ;

And would sigh at the tale
Of sunk Lyonnesse,
As a wind-tugged tress
Flapped her cheek like a flail ;
Or listen at whiles
With a thought-bound brow
To the murmuring miles
She is far from now.

Yet her shade, maybe,
Will creep underground
Till it catch the sound
Of that western sea
As it swells and sobs
Where she once domiciled,
And joy in its throbs
With the heart of a child.

# WITHOUT CEREMONY

It was your way, my dear,
To vanish without a word
When callers, friends, or kin
Had left, and I hastened in
To rejoin you, as I inferred.

And when you'd a mind to career
Off anywhere—say to town—
You were all on a sudden gone
Before I had thought thereon,
Or noticed your trunks were down.

So, now that you disappear
For ever in that swift style,
Your meaning seems to me
Just as it used to be :
" Good-bye is not worth while ! "

# LAMENT

How she would have loved
A party to-day !—
Bright-hatted and gloved,
With table and tray
And chairs on the lawn
Her smiles would have shone
With welcomings. . . . But
She is shut, she is shut
    From friendship's spell
    In the jailing shell
    Of her tiny cell.

Or she would have reigned
At a dinner to-night
With ardours unfeigned,
And a generous delight ;
All in her abode
She'd have freely bestowed
On her guests. . . . But alas,
She is shut under grass
    Where no cups flow,
    Powerless to know
    That it might be so.

313

And she would have sought
With a child's eager glance
The shy snowdrops brought
By the new year's advance,
And peered in the rime
Of Candlemas-time
For crocuses . . . chanced
It that she were not tranced
　　　From sights she loved best ;
　　　Wholly possessed
　　　By an infinite rest !

And we are here staying
Amid these stale things,
Who care not for gaying,
And those junketings
That used so to joy her,
And never to cloy her
As us they cloy ! . . . But
She is shut, she is shut
　　　From the cheer of them, dead
　　　To all done and said
　　　In her yew-arched bed.

# THE HAUNTER

HE does not think that I haunt here nightly:
    How shall I let him know
That whither his fancy sets him wandering
    I, too, alertly go ?—
Hover and hover a few feet from him
    Just as I used to do,
But cannot answer the words he lifts me—
    Only listen thereto !

When I could answer he did not say them :
    When I could let him know
How I would like to join in his journeys
    Seldom he wished to go.
Now that he goes and wants me with him
    More than he used to do,
Never he sees my faithful phantom
    Though he speaks thereto.

Yes, I companion him to places
    Only dreamers know,
Where the shy hares print long paces,
    Where the night rooks go ;
Into old aisles where the past is all to him,
    Close as his shade can do,
Always lacking the power to call to him,
    Near as I reach thereto !

What a good haunter I am, O tell him !
    Quickly make him know
If he but sigh since my loss befell him
    Straight to his side I go.
Tell him a faithful one is doing
    All that love can do
Still that his path may be worth pursuing,
    And to bring peace thereto.

# THE VOICE

Woman much missed, how you call to me, call to
      me,
Saying that now you are not as you were
When you had changed from the one who was
      all to me,
But as at first, when our day was fair.

Can it be you that I hear ? Let me view you,
      then,
Standing as when I drew near to the town
Where you would wait for me : yes, as I knew
      you then,
Even to the original air-blue gown !

Or is it only the breeze, in its listlessness
Travelling across the wet mead to me here,
You being ever dissolved to wan wistlessness,
Heard no more again far or near ?

    Thus I ; faltering forward,
    Leaves around me falling,
Wind oozing thin through the thorn from
      norward,
    And the woman calling.

*December 1912*

# HIS VISITOR

I COME across from Mellstock while the moon
   wastes weaker
To behold where I lived with you for twenty
   years and more :
I shall go in the gray, at the passing of the mail-
   train,
And need no setting open of the long familiar
   door
    As before.

The change I notice in my once own quarters !
A formal-fashioned border where the daisies
   used to be,
The rooms new painted, and the pictures
   altered,
And other cups and saucers, and no cosy nook for
   tea
    As with me.

I discern the dim faces of the sleep-wrapt
   servants ;
They are not those who tended me through
   feeble hours and strong,
But strangers quite, who never knew my rule
   here,
Who never saw me painting, never heard my
   softling song
    Float along.

318

So I don't want to linger in this re-decked
     dwelling,
I feel too uneasy at the contrasts I behold,
And I make again for Mellstock to return here
     never,
And rejoin the roomy silence, and the mute and
     manifold
     Souls of old.

*1913*

# A CIRCULAR

As " legal representative "
I read a missive not my own,
On new designs the senders give
    For clothes, in tints as shown.

Here figure blouses, gowns for tea,
And presentation-trains of state,
Charming ball-dresses, millinery,
    Warranted up to date.

And this gay-pictured, spring-time shout
Of Fashion, hails what lady proud ?
Her who before last year ebbed out
    Was costumed in a shroud.

# A DREAM OR NO

Why go to Saint-Juliot ? What's Juliot to me ?
    Some strange necromancy
    But charmed me to fancy
That much of my life claims the spot as its key.

Yes. I have had dreams of that place in the West,
    And a maiden abiding
    Thereat as in hiding ;
Fair-eyed and white-shouldered, broad-browed
    and brown-tressed.

And of how, coastward bound on a night long
    ago,
    There lonely I found her,
    The sea-birds around her,
And other than nigh things uncaring to know.

So sweet her life there (in my thought has it
    seemed)
    That quickly she drew me
    To take her unto me,
And lodge her long years with me. Such have I
    dreamed.

But nought of that maid from Saint-Juliot I see ;
     Can she ever have been here,
     And shed her life's sheen here,
The woman I thought a long housemate with
     me ?

Does there even a place like Saint-Juliot exist ?
     Or a Vallency Valley
     With stream and leafed alley,
Or Beeny, or Bos with its flounce flinging mist ?

*February 1913*

## AFTER A JOURNEY

Hereto I come to view a voiceless ghost ;
   Whither, O whither will its whim now draw
      me ?
Up the cliff, down, till I'm lonely, lost,
   And the unseen waters' ejaculations awe me.
Where you will next be there's no knowing,
   Facing round about me everywhere,
      With your nut-coloured hair,
And gray eyes, and rose-flush coming and going.

Yes : I have re-entered your olden haunts at
      last ;
   Through the years, through the dead scenes I
      have tracked you ;
What have you now found to say of our past—
   Scanned across the dark space wherein I have
      lacked you ?
Summer gave us sweets, but autumn wrought
      division ?
   Things were not lastly as firstly well
      With us twain, you tell ?
But all's closed now, despite Time's derision.

I see what you are doing : you are leading me on
   To the spots we knew when we haunted here
      together,

The waterfall, above which the mist-bow shone
 At the then fair hour in the then fair weather,
And the cave just under, with a voice still so
  hollow
 That it seems to call out to me from forty years
  ago,
  When you were all aglow,
And not the thin ghost that I now fraily follow !

Ignorant of what there is flitting here to see,
 The waked birds preen and the seals flop
  lazily ;
Soon you will have, Dear, to vanish from me,
 For the stars close their shutters and the dawn
  whitens hazily.
Trust me, I mind not, though Life lours,
 The bringing me here ; nay, bring me here
  again !
  I am just the same as when
Our days were a joy, and our paths through
  flowers.

*Pentargan Bay*

# A DEATH-DAY RECALLED

BEENY did not quiver,
  Juliot grew not gray,
Thin Vallency's river
  Held its wonted way.
Bos seemed not to utter
  Dimmest note of dirge,
Targan mouth a mutter
  To its creamy surge.

Yet though these, unheeding,
  Listless, passed the hour
Of her spirit's speeding,
  She had, in her flower,
Sought and loved the places—
  Much and often pined
For their lonely faces
  When in towns confined.

Why did not Vallency
  In his purl deplore
One whose haunts were whence he
  Drew his limpid store ?
Why did Bos not thunder,
  Targan apprehend
Body and Breath were sunder
  Of their former friend ?

# BEENY CLIFF

*March 1870—March 1913*

### I

O THE opal and the sapphire of that wandering
    western sea,
And the woman riding high above with bright
    hair flapping free—
The woman whom I loved so, and who loyally
    loved me.

### II

The pale mews plained below us, and the waves
    seemed far away
In a nether sky, engrossed in saying their
    ceaseless babbling say,
As we laughed light-heartedly aloft on that
    clear-sunned March day.

### III

A little cloud then cloaked us, and there flew an
    irised rain,
And the Atlantic dyed its levels with a dull
    misfeatured stain,
And then the sun burst out again, and purples
    prinked the main.

326

## IV

—Still in all its chasmal beauty bulks old Beeny
to the sky,
And shall she and I not go there once again now
March is nigh,
And the sweet things said in that March say
anew there by and by ?

## V

What if still in chasmal beauty looms that wild
weird western shore,
The woman now is—elsewhere—whom the
ambling pony bore,
And nor knows nor cares for Beeny, and will
laugh there nevermore.

# AT CASTLE BOTEREL

As I drive to the junction of lane and highway,
  And the drizzle bedrenches the waggonette,
I look behind at the fading byway,
  And see on its slope, now glistening wet,
    Distinctly yet

Myself and a girlish form benighted
  In dry March weather. We climb the road
Beside a chaise. We had just alighted
  To ease the sturdy pony's load
    When he sighed and slowed.

What we did as we climbed, and what we talked
    of
  Matters not much, nor to what it led,—
Something that life will not be balked of
  Without rude reason till hope is dead,
    And feeling fled.

It filled but a minute. But was there ever
  A time of such quality, since or before,
In that hill's story ? To one mind never,
  Though it has been climbed, foot-swift, foot-
    sore,
    By thousands more.

Primaeval rocks form the road's steep border,
   And much have they faced there, first and last,
Of the transitory in Earth's long order ;
   But what they record in colour and cast
      Is—that we two passed.

And to me, though Time's unflinching rigour,
   In mindless rote, has ruled from sight
The substance now, one phantom figure
   Remains on the slope, as when that night
      Saw us alight.

I look and see it there, shrinking, shrinking,
   I look back at it amid the rain
For the very last time ; for my sand is sinking,
   And I shall traverse old love's domain
      Never again.

*March 1913*

# PLACES

NOBODY says : Ah, that is the place
Where chanced, in the hollow of years ago,
What none of the Three Towns cared to know—
The birth of a little girl of grace—
The sweetest the house saw, first or last ;
      Yet it was so
      On that day long past.

Nobody thinks : There, there she lay
In a room by the Hoe, like the bud of a flower,
And listened, just after the bedtime hour,
To the stammering chimes that used to play
The quaint Old Hundred-and-Thirteenth tune
      In Saint Andrew's tower
      Night, morn, and noon.

Nobody calls to mind that here
Upon Boterel Hill, where the waggoners skid,
With cheeks whose airy flush outbid
Fresh fruit in bloom, and free of fear,
She cantered down, as if she must fall
      (Though she never did),
      To the charm of all.

Nay : one there is to whom these things,
That nobody else's mind calls back,
Have a savour that scenes in being lack,
And a presence more than the actual brings ;
To whom to-day is beneaped and stale,
      And its urgent clack
      But a vapid tale.

*Plymouth, March 1913*

# THE PHANTOM HORSEWOMAN

### I

QUEER are the ways of a man I know :
        He comes and stands
        In a careworn craze,
        And looks at the sands
        And the seaward haze
        With moveless hands
        And face and gaze,
        Then turns to go  . . .
And what does he see when he gazes so ?

### II

They say he sees as an instant thing
        More clear than to-day,
        A sweet soft scene
        That was once in play
        By that briny green ;
        Yes, notes alway
        Warm, real, and keen,
        What his back years bring—
A phantom of his own figuring.

332

### III

Of this vision of his they might say more :
      Not only there
      Does he see this sight,
      But everywhere
      In his brain—day, night,
      As if on the air
      It were drawn rose-bright—
      Yea, far from that shore
Does he carry this vision of heretofore :

### IV

A ghost-girl-rider. And though, toil-tried,
      He withers daily,
      Time touches her not,
      But she still rides gaily
      In his rapt thought
      On that shagged and shaly
      Atlantic spot,
      And as when first eyed
Draws rein and sings to the swing of the tide.

*1913*

# THE SPELL OF THE ROSE

" I MEAN to build a hall anon,
  And shape two turrets there,
  And a broad newelled stair,
And a cool well for crystal water ;
  Yes ; I will build a hall anon,
  Plant roses love shall feed upon,
  And apple-trees and pear."

He set to build the manor-hall,
  And shaped the turrets there,
  And the broad newelled stair,
And the cool well for crystal water ;
  He built for me that manor-hall,
  And planted many trees withal,
  But no rose anywhere.

And as he planted never a rose
  That bears the flower of love,
  Though other flowers throve
Some heart-bane moved our souls to sever
  Since he had planted never a rose ;
  And misconceits raised horrid shows,
  And agonies came thereof.

" I'll mend these miseries," then said I,
    And so, at dead of night,
    I went and, screened from sight,
That nought should keep our souls in severance,
    I set a rose-bush. " This," said I,
    " May end divisions dire and wry,
    And long-drawn days of blight."

But I was called from earth—yea, called
    Before my rose-bush grew ;
    And would that now I knew
What feels he of the tree I planted,
    And whether, after I was called
    To be a ghost, he, as of old,
    Gave me his heart anew !

Perhaps now blooms that queen of trees
    I set but saw not grow,
    And he, beside its glow—
Eyes couched of the mis-vision that blurred me—
    Ay, there beside that queen of trees
    He sees me as I was, though sees
    Too late to tell me so !

## ST LAUNCE'S REVISITED

Slip back, Time !
Yet again I am nearing
Castle and keep, uprearing
  Gray, as in my prime.

At the inn
Smiling nigh, why is it
Not as on my visit
  When hope and I were twin ?

Groom and jade
Whom I found here, moulder ;
Strange the tavern-holder,
  Strange the tap-maid.

Here I hired
Horse and man for bearing
Me on my wayfaring
  To the door desired.

Evening gloomed
As I journeyed forward
To the faces shoreward,
  Till their dwelling loomed.

    If again
Towards the Atlantic sea there
I should speed, they'd be there
    Surely now as then ?  . . .

    Why waste thought,
When I know them vanished
Under earth ; yea, banished
    Ever into nought !

## WHERE THE PICNIC WAS

WHERE we made the fire
In the summer time
Of branch and briar
On the hill to the sea,
I slowly climb
Through winter mire,
And scan and trace
The forsaken place
Quite readily.

Now a cold wind blows,
And the grass is gray,
But the spot still shows
As a burnt circle—aye,
And stick-ends, charred,
Still strew the sward
Whereon I stand,
Last relic of the band
Who came that day !

Yes, I am here
Just as last year,
And the sea breathes brine
From its strange straight line
Up hither, the same

As when we four came.
—But two have wandered far
From this grassy rise
Into urban roar
Where no picnics are,
And one—has shut her eyes
For evermore.

# NOTES

Abbreviations:

CP—*Collected Poems of Thomas Hardy*, 1928 edition
DF—*The Dynasts*, Part First
DS—*The Dynasts*, Part Second
DT—*The Dynasts*, Part Third
QC—*The Famous Tragedy of the Queen of Cornwall*

PAGE

341

234 *In Tenebris*   Entitled "In Tenebris II" in CP

257 *Jezreel*   Stanza 3 line 1 appears in CP as "Faintly marked they the words 'Throw her down!' rise from Night eerily"

259 *In Time of "The Breaking of Nations"*   Stanza 3 line 3 appears in CP as "War's annals will fade into night"

260 *The Night of Trafalgar*   The song ends Act V Scene VII of DF. Hardy included a footnote to explain "the Back-sea met the Front-sea" (stanza 1 line 2): "In those days the hind-part of the harbour adjoining this scene was so named, and at high tides the waves washed across the isthmus at a point called 'The Narrows.'"

262 *Albuera*   The song by the Chorus of the Pities ends Act VI Scene IV of DS. It was added to the other six excerpts from *The Dynasts* when Hardy revised his *Selected Poems* and appears in no other Hardy collection.

264 *Hussar's Song*   The song by the Hussar Sergeant commemorating the "Budmouth Dears" ends Act II Scene I of DT. Hardy explained the "sling-jacket" (stanza 4 line 3) with a footnote: "Hussars, it may be remembered, used to wear a pelisse, dolman, or 'sling-jacket' (as the men called it), which hung loosely over the shoulder. The writer is able to recall the picturesque effect of this uniform."

266 *"My Love's Gone A-Fighting"*   The song ends Act V Scene VI of DT.

267 *The Eve of Waterloo*   The chorus ends Act VI Scene VIII of DT. Stanza last line 1 appears as "And each soul shivers as sinks his head"

269 *Chorus of the Pities*   This homage to the "Immanent Will" appears in the "After Scene" of DT.

271 *Last Chorus*   The song constitutes the concluding passages of DT. The opening question of *The Dynasts* is "What of the Immanent Will and Its designs?" It should be observed that the opening poem of *Chosen Poems* poses a parallel "eternal question" and that both panoramas of dramatic personae end on the identical ray of hope.

# INDEX OF TITLES

The letters in parentheses adjacent to each title indicate the collection in which the poem first appeared. The nine poems originally published in *Selected Poems* were later reprinted in *Moments of Vision*.

# INDEX OF FIRST LINES